There is no frigate like a book
  To take us lands away,
    Nor any coursers like a page
    Of prancing poetry.
      This traverse may the poorest take,
      Without oppress of toll;
        How frugal is the chariot
        That bears the human soul!

—EMILY DICKINSON

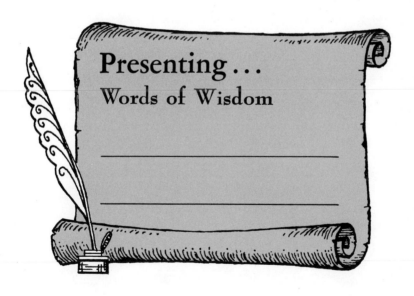

Presenting...

Words of Wisdom

_____

_____

WORDS
OF
WISDOM

Selections from many sources
providing
reading for casual enjoyment
thoughts for patient perusal
and
nonsense for pleasant pastime

Edited by
THOMAS C. JONES

J. G. FERGUSON PUBLISHING COMPANY
CHICAGO

EDITOR'S COMMENT AND ACKNOWLEDGMENTS

Any selection of reading as widely varied as this becomes almost a literary lottery. One might gain the impression from an examination of the contents that little or no plan of selection guided the editor. This is almost correct in the sense that the material had to qualify only on the basis of being enlightening, provocative, amusing, or tastefully expressed. Very few long articles, essays or poems have been included because the prime aim is to keep the material "casual."

Some rather unusual sources were used in seeking fresh "new" material. In fact, some articles are new only in the sense that they have been dug out of the forgotten pages of time. Almanacs and periodicals of the 18th and 19th Centuries are rich in personal eyewitness stories of historic events. For example, the story of the Sergeant at the Battle of Princeton, entitled *A Patriot's Story,* is an eyewitness account by one who was there, describing in his own words the privations of the Revolutionary Army. The first-hand contact with George Washington mentioned in the article gives insight into the greatness of this giant among national heroes whose personal contributions to American freedom are sometimes forgotten with the passing of generations.

Likewise, the intimate account of the events surrounding the origin of *The Star-Spangled Banner* comes from a source as authentic as one can find, short of the author himself. In this case Roger B. Taney, a Chief Justice of the United States Supreme Court and brother-in-law of Francis Scott Key, narrates the details as he knew them to be. The thrill of knowing how this great national anthem was inspired under fire makes it just a little more impressive.

James Audubon's description of the Ohio River on an autumn day in the 1830's gives the reader a kinship with a period of our history that is rapidly slipping away. The countryside of that era, as seen through the eyes of the great naturalist and painter, takes on a freshness that only this kind of report can impart.

The early history of baseball as described by A. G. Spalding, one of the game's first stars and later an important developer of sporting equipment and publisher of official rules, gives an insight into the beginning of major league baseball. It is interesting to observe that rather than being spawned by promoters, it was an outgrowth of inter-city competition between rival towns which wanted to outbid each other to get the best players.

The *Rules of Warfare* as set forth by Prince Machiavelli in the 16th Century are interesting today in that they are, for the most part, still fundamentally sound. Despite the dramatic changes in weapons and firepower, the basics remain the same. The sophisticated mobile armies of today rely on very much the same tactics that were employed at the time of the spear and the crossbow.

The poems and verses were chosen largely for the anti-poetry type of reader, who sometimes can be seduced into the reading of poetry if it fits a mood or covers a subject of popular interest. Several poems by Eugene Field, known as a child's poet, have been selected because they carry a message and have broad general appeal. The same can be said for the poems of Joyce Kilmer. Although basically not a child's poet, his work is readily appreciated by most readers.

In Dr. Thomas Dooley's short life of dedication to mankind he brought relief from suffering to some of the deprived people of Southeast Asia. His philosophy carries a message for all mankind in this period of worldwide restlessness and wars and threats of war. Tom Dooley's Vietnamese experiences began before any great involvement by the United States, and he brought to that unhappy area an example of the assistance that can be generally available to those people if they can somehow work out a viable political destiny.

The Creative Department of Brown and Bigelow, St. Paul, Minnesota, has been helpful in planning this volume and in furnishing much of the art. Other illustrations are the work of Kay Lovelace Smith. Harriet Helmer, as editorial assistant, has been helpful in all phases of production. Type design has been the work of Walter Luchman and page layout has been ably handled by Al Josephson. A-1 Composition Company of Chicago and Photopress, Inc., lithographer, of Broadview, Illinois, have been responsible for the overall physical quality, with an assist from A. C. Engdahl and Company, Inc., bookbinders, of Bensenville, Illinois. To all of these people and firms the publisher is extremely grateful.

Many sources have provided a variety of reading that should be moderately enjoyable to some readers and perhaps thoroughly amusing to others. We are indebted to many authors and publishers for the privilege of reprinting, as well as for reference. We wish to thank the authors and publishers in the following list for their magnificent cooperation. If through oversight or error material is improperly credited or not credited at all, this will be corrected on future printings if called to our attention.

Permissions have been granted by the following: DOUBLE-DAY & CO., INC.—"Citizen of the World," copyright 1914 by Aline Kilmer; "Old Poets," copyright 1914 by John Adams Thayer Corporation; "Main Street," copyright 1917 by George H. Doran Company, all from the book, POEMS, ESSAYS and LETTERS by Joyce Kilmer. Reprinted by permission of Doubleday & Company, Inc. "Dog in a Car," copyright 1936 by David McCord, from the book, A STAR BY DAY by David McCord. Reprinted by permission of Doubleday & Company, Inc. Excerpt from *Clarence Darrow for the Defense* by Irving Stone, copyright 1941 by Irving Stone. Excerpt from *Recollections and Letters of Gen-*

25—*Medical Men In The American Revolution.* The Bowen-Merrill Company—*Rhymes of Childhood* by James Whitcomb Riley. The Century Company—*The Many-Sided Franklin* by Paul Leicester Ford. The Christian Herald—*Best Things From American Literature*, edited by Irving Bacheller. Cowperthwait & Co.—*Ten Years Among The Mail Bags* by J. Holbrook. Curtis and Cameron—*The Quest of the Holy Grail* by Ferris Greenslet. The Dial Press—*Alexander Hamilton and The Founding of The Nation*, edited by Richard B. Morris. David Douglas—*Songs of the Edinburgh Angling Club.* J. T. Hackett—*My Commonplace Book.* J. E. Haynes—*The Discovery of Yellowstone Park* by Nathaniel Pitt Langford. Houghton Mifflin & Company—*A Multitude of Counsellors.* Hurd and Houghton—*Birds and Poets, With Other Papers* by John Burroughs. Langtree and O'Sullivan—*United States Magazine and Democratic Review.* J. B. Lippincott & Company—*Prose Quotations From Socrates to Macaulay.* The Macmillan Company —*Historic Mackinac* by Edwin O. Wood (All efforts to receive permission have been exhausted.) The McClure Company—*The Story of the White House* by Esther Singleton. Moffat, Yard and Company—*Flag Day*, edited by Robert Haven Schauffler. The New England Almanack of 1812. *No Cross, No Crown* by William Penn. David Nutt—MACHIAVELLI, Volume I, *The Art of War* and *The Prince.* The Old South Association—*Old South Leaflets* (No. 179). *Proverbs and Common Sayings from the Chinese* by Arthur H. Smith. G. P. Putnam's Sons—*Breaking the Wilderness* by Frederick S. Dellenbaugh. The Reilly & Britton Company—*The Little Book of Cheer*, compiled and edited with an introduction by Wallace and Frances Rice. Roberts Brothers—*Letters of Emily Dickinson*, edited by Mabel Loomis Todd. *Sawdust and Spangles* by W. C. Coup. Charles Scribner's Sons—*Mining Camps*, A Study in American Frontier Government by Charles Howard Shinn; *Patrick Henry*, Life, Correspondence and Speeches by William Wirt Henry; *The Poems of Eugene Field* by Eugene Field. Sholl's Colonial Cafeteria, Washington, D. C.—*Friendship is a Chain of Gold.* J. S. Snoddy—*A Little Book of Missouri Verse.* Spalding Guide of 1905. Sully and Kleinteich — *One Thousand Literary Questions and Answers* by Mary Eleanor Kramer. The Tennessee Farmer—*The Road to Success.* Veterans of Foreign Wars of the United States—Pamphlets issued by Americanization Department: *Abraham Lincoln's Second Inaugural Address;* The Autobiography of Abraham Lincoln; I Am Not a Virginian But an American, Patrick Henry, Statesman-Patriot; John Adams—Inaugural Address; The Monroe Doctrine, also Jefferson's Letter to Monroe.

TABLE OF CONTENTS

Living Day By Day

Brave Words

The Spirit of Sport

Humor

Mostly For Men

The Women's World

Business Brevities

LIVING DAY BY DAY

I serenade thee dear World!

From: *Poem Outlines by* SIDNEY LANIER
Copyright 1908 by Charles Scribner's Sons

Like to the grasshopper in the tall grass,
That sings to the mate he cannot see yet while,
I sing to thee, dear World;
For thou art my Mate, and peradventure thou wilt
    come; I wish to see thee.
Like to the lover under the window of his Love,
I serenade thee, dear World;
For thou art asleep and thou art my Love,
And perhaps thou wilt awake and show me thine eyes
And the beauty of thy face out of the window of thy
    house of Time.

How happy is the little stone
That rambles in the road alone,
And doesn't care about careers,
And exigencies never fears;
Whose coat of elemental brown
A passing universe put on;
And independent as the sun,
Associates, or glows alone,
Fulfilling absolute decree
In casual simplicity.

—EMILY DICKINSON
From *Letters of Emily Dickinson*

Friendship is a Chain of Gold

A poem adorning the wall of Sholl's Colonial Cafeteria, Washington, D.C.

Friendship is a chain of gold
Shaped in God's all perfect mold,
Each link a smile, a laugh, a tear,
A grip of the hand, a word of cheer.

As steadfast as the ages roll
Binding closer soul to soul,
No matter how far or heavy the load,
Sweet is the journey of friendship's road.

It is our joy in life to find
At every turning of the road
The strong arm of a comrade kind
To help us onward with our load.

And since we have no gold to give
And love alone must make amends,
Our only prayer is while we live
God make us worthy of our friends.

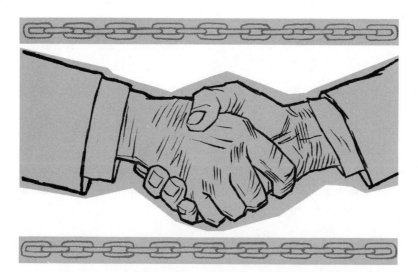

Twenty-one Maxims for Better Living

by GEORGE WASHINGTON

1. Sleep not when others speak, sit not when others stand, speak not when you should hold your peace, and walk not when others stop.

2. Let your discourse with men of business be short and comprehensive.

3. In writing or speaking, give to every person his due title, according to his degree and the custom of the place.

4. Strive not with your superiors in argument, but always submit your judgment to others with modesty.

5. When about to advise or reprehend any one, consider whether it ought to be in public or private, presently or at some other time; also in what terms to do it; and in reproving, show no signs of choler, but do it with sweetness and mildness.

6. Take all admonitions thankfully, in whatsoever place given; but afterwards, not being culpable, take a time or place convenient to let him know it that gave them.

7. Be not hasty to believe flying reports, to the disparagement of any one.

8. Associate yourself with men of good quality if you esteem your own reputation, for it is better to be alone than in bad company.

9. Let your conversation be without malice or envy, for it is a sign of a tractable and commendable nature, and in all cases of passion admit reason to govern.

10. Speak not injurious words neither in jest or in earnest. Scoff at none, although they give occasion.

11. Detract not from others, but neither be excessive in commending.

12. If two contend together, take not the part of either unconstrained, and be not obstinate in your opinion; in things indifferent be of the major side.

13. When another speaks, be attentive yourself, and disturb not the audience. If any hesitate in his words help him not, and answer him not till his speech be ended.

14. Undertake not what you cannot perform, but be careful to keep your promise.

15. In disputes, be not so desirous to overcome that you do not give liberty to each one to deliver his opinion, and submit to the judgment of the major part especially if they are judges of the dispute.

16. Be not tedious in discourse, make not many digressions, nor repeat often the same matter of discourse.

17. Speak no evil of the absent, for it is unjust.

18. Be not angry at the table whatever happens, and if you have reason to be so, show it not; put on a cheerful countenance, especially if there be strangers, for good humor makes one dish a feast.

19. Seat not yourself at the upper end of the table, but if it be your due or the master of the house will have it so, contend not lest you should trouble the company.

20. Let your recreations be manful, not sinful.

21. Labor to keep alive in your breast the little spark of celestial fire called consience.

If any little word of mine
   May make a life the brighter;
If any little song of mine
   May make a heart the lighter;
God help me to speak the little word
   And take my bit of singing
And drop it in some lonely vale,
   To set the echoes ringing.

ANONYMOUS

From the New England Almanack of 1812

Farmers! I wish you a happy New Year! But by this wish I do not mean that you should be keeping Thanksgiving or Christmas all the time. The old proverb says "enough is as good as a feast." Therefore your happiness will much depend on your mixing some other matters with your jollity... Joe, I see, has brought a merry book home with him from market. It makes little Dick grin as he sits in the chimney corner, or in the recess of the oven door. Well, it is evening so let the boys read—a little mirth will do them no harm—I wish they would read more.

It would not be amiss if the girls had a few books such as would keep them to be discreet, chaste, keepers at home, not tattlers, not busy bodies—concerning themselves more about other people's matters than their own. This I say for their benefit—not that I don't think they are pretty girls on the whole, and in due time I heartily wish them good husbands. But when the young men come to see them, it will be a great recommendation if they hear the spinning wheels busily humming.

The December entry in the Almanack gives the following advice:

You will now have time to attend to the education of your children, to settle your accounts and to recollect that the state of the world would be better than it is now if everybody would obey the Apostolic injunction to owe no man anything. When you survey the products of the late season you may also say with the wise man—"I know that there is no good in them but for a man to rejoice and to do good in his life, and also that every man should eat and drink and enjoy the good of all his labor—it is the gift of God."

You cannot better improve in your children a desire for learning than by indulging them with books calculated to awaken a thirst for knowledge and which at the same time contain incentives to virtuous actions.

Necessity never made a good bargain. A little
house well filled, a little field well tilled,
and a little wife well will'd are great riches.

Of the diseases this year

This year the stone-blind shall see but very little;
the deaf shall hear but poorly, and the dumb shan't
speak very plain. And it's much if my dame Bridget
talks at all this year. Whole flocks, herds and
droves of sheep, swine and oxen, cocks, hens, ducks
and drakes and geese and ganders shall go to pot;
but the mortality shall not be altogether so great
among cats, dogs and horses.

Of the fruits of the earth

I find that this will be a plentiful year of all
manner of good things to those who have enough; but
the orange trees in Greenland will go near to fare
the worse for the cold. As for oats, they'll be a
great help to horses.

"Lend money to an enemy and thou'lt gain him;
to a friend, and thou'lt lose him."

Keep your eyes wide open before marriage, half shut
afterwards.

A young lady sent the following lines to her lover,
whose name was Nott, a few weeks before their
marriage. The mystical knot was fastened soon after
the discerning lover deciphered its import.

Why urge, dear sir, a bashful maid,
  To change her single lot?
When well you know, I've often said,
  In truth, I love you, Nott.
For all your pain I do, Nott, care,
  And trust me, on my life,
Though you had millions, I declare,
  I would, Nott, be your wife.

*   *   *

A little work, a little play
To keep us going—and so good-day!

A little warmth, a little light
Of love's bestowing—and so, good-night!

A little fun, to match the sorrow
Of each day's growing—and so, good-morrow!

A little trust that when we die
We reap our sowing! And so—goodbye!

George du Maurier

The Joy of the Rebel

an expression *by* SIDNEY LANIER from *Poem Outlines*

A man does not reach any stature of manhood until like Moses he kills an Egyptian (*i.e.*, murders some oppressive prejudice of the all-crushing Tyrant Society or Custom or Orthodoxy) and flies into the desert of his own soul. There among the rocks and sands, over which at any rate the sun rises clear each day, he slowly and with great agony settles his relation with men and manners and powers outside, and begins to look with his own eyes, and first knows the unspeakable joy of the outcast's kiss upon the hand of sweet, naked Truth.

But let not the young man go to killing his Egyptian too soon: wait till you know all the Egyptians can teach you: wait till you are master of the technics of the time; then grave, and resolute, and aware of consequences, shape your course.

DOG IN A CAR

by DAVID McCORD

From: *Jubilee*, One Hundred Years of the Atlantic
selected and edited by Edward Weeks and Emily Flint
Copyright 1957, Little, Brown and Company

He grins a little as they drive him by.
Of what his nose needs there's a fresh supply
Round every corner, up the rainy field:
He has no daily walk of equal yield.
His head hangs out, his tongue out farther still;
His bark is bolder from that window sill.
His nose is longer on the modern breeze—
His father being Scotch, not Pekingese.

A lesser breed on leash or running loose
Would find his comradeship of little use;
A dog transported by the family Ford
Rides far beyond the days he loved or warred.
His ancestors on purely urban smells
Leaned hard enough, but they had nothing else.
They hadn't won to his synthetic taste:
Investigation kept them out of haste.

You drive a dog from state to other state;
His senses meet with scents he can't relate.
He hasn't time. His little nostrils twitch.
Was that a rabbit, mole, or brindle bitch?
His eye grows bright. He reaches out in space.
The local brothers hardly see his face.
He's whirling through a night of strange impact—
Of atavistic cats he once attacked.

Which Flag Is Yours?

What kind of a flag are you marching under? There is the blue flag of Truth; its colors are loyal, and its principles are good; why not join its ranks? There is the green flag of Hope; that is a grand old flag! Its defenders are ever looking forward to a good time coming; their hearts are loyal and their strength of purpose never falters. There is the red flag of Love; it leads to victory, and its followers have the charity that "covereth a multitude of sins." There is the yellow flag of Courage; they who carry this golden banner are firm, resolute, and dauntless. There is the black flag of Despair; the mud-brown flag of Malice; the gray flag of Discontent; the rosy flag of Happiness; and the royal purple flag of Kingly Kindness; while a little higher than them all floats the pure white folds of the flag whereon is inscribed Faith, Purity, and Peace.

Choose your flag; one, or more, belongs to you; your life-march is going on underneath it, and you are under orders, and keeping time to the music of its band. See to it that you have chosen the right color, and that your commander belongs to the King's great Army.

My half-day's work is done,
　And this is all my part,—
I give a patient God
　My patient heart;
And grasp His banner still,
　Though all the blue be dim;
These stripes as well as stars
　Lead after Him.

MARY WOOLSEY HOWLAND

Where Shall Wisdom Be Found?

But where shall wisdom be found? and where is the place of understanding?

Man knoweth not the price thereof; neither is it found in the land of the living.

The depth saith, It is not with me: and the sea saith, It is not with me.

It cannot be gotten for gold, neither shall silver be weighed for the price thereof.

It cannot be valued with the gold of Ophir, with the precious onyx, or the sapphire.

The gold and the crystal cannot equal it; and the exchange of it shall not be for jewels of fine gold.

No mention shall be made of coral, or of pearls: for the price of wisdom is above rubies.

The topaz of Ethiopia shall not equal it, neither shall it be valued with pure gold.

Whence cometh wisdom? and where is the place of understanding?

Seeing it is hid from the eyes of all living, and kept close from the fowls of the air.

Destruction and death say, We have heard the fame thereof with our ears.

God understandeth the way thereof, and He knoweth the place thereof.

For he looketh to the ends of the earth, and seeth under the whole heaven;

To make the weight for the winds; and he weigheth the waters by measure.

When he made a decree for the rain, and a way for the lightning of the thunder:

Then did he see it, and declare it; he prepared it, yea, and searched it out.

And unto man He saith, Behold the fear of the Lord, that is wisdom: and to depart from evil is understanding.—JOB 28:12–28.

Ancient Chinese Proverbs

From *Proverbs and Common Sayings from the Chinese*
by ARTHUR H. SMITH

A foot of jade is of no value; an inch of time should be highly prized.

Harmonious above, united below; the husband sings, the wife accompanies.

The workman who wishes to do his work well must first sharpen the tools.

If a man take no thought for what is distant, he will find sorrow near at hand.

Riches adorn a house, and virtue adorns a person.

In all things success depends on preparation; without it there is failure.

That which happens without man's causing it to happen is the decree of heaven.

The feeling of pity is common to all men; the feeling of shame and dislike is common to all men; the feeling of reverence and respect is common to all; and the knowledge of right and wrong is common to all.

Words which are simple, but far-reaching in meaning, are good words.

The family which stores up virtue will have an exuberance of happiness; the family which stores up vice will have overwhelming calamity.

When three men are of one heart, yellow earth is turned to gold.

On entering a country, inquire what is forbidden; on entering a village, inquire what are the customs; on entering a private house, inquire for the personal names of the family. (In China names were personal things. Even a son could not speak his father's name.)

Do not listen to unsubstantiated words; do not adopt undeliberated plans.

Relatives should have equality in condition; friends must be on a par in their property.

· · · · · · · · ·

When sisters-in-law are joined in heart
No family comes to ill;
When sons all act a filial part
It works like a harmony pill.

The man who rules his appetite
Will always keep his spirits light,
But many anxious thoughts combine
The vital force to undermine;
Refrain from wine and save your health,
Nor yield to wrath that wastes your wealth.

Three days the newly married bride
In strict seclusion ought to hide;
With dainty hands then sallies forth
To mix her trial pot of broth.
In life as is known to most,
The husband's mother rules the roost,
But to the new made bride alone
This lady's tastes are all unknown.
Lest, wrongly mixed, her soup she waste
She makes her husband's sister taste.

Solace to the Weight-Watcher

Long not for dainties rich and rare,
For dangers lie in ambush there;
Along the surface of the tongue
The nerves of taste are finely strung.
Consider this important fact—
No matter what the food you eat,
Once past this gustatory tract
Who can distinguish sour from sweet?

A stick that is crooked, though ironed out straight,
        is as crooked at last as before,
And the Wolf that you train to behave like a dog
        will hardly stand guard at your door.
The Raven, though powdered and washed till he's white,
        not for long will appear to be clean,
And the pure Fairy Crane when you've dyed him in ink,
        will never look fit to be seen.
The juice of the Wormwood, with honey though mixed, yet its
        taste it is hopeless to sweeten;
So Melons and Fruits that are picked while they are green,
        will never be good to be eaten.
To do as he should, whatsoever is good, is in none
        but the wise man's reach,
But whom Heaven at his birth has endowed as a fool,
        'tis a waste of instruction to teach.

"Things Are Never Quite So Bad As We Imagine"

Keep up a brave spirit; things are never quite so bad as we imagine they may be. God always lets in the sunshine somewhere. Hope on; no matter how dark the way seems, it is better farther on. Do not be discouraged; if business is dull, if troubles overwhelm you, if you have losses and crosses, or if you are deceived and disappointed, go on hoping and trusting; there is a good time coming for you! Take hold of the every-day duties, and if they are not to your taste, and of your seeking, honor them, anyway. By doing these things well, you shall be found worthy of greater ones. Work and hope; your Better Day will dawn.

The Glory of the Book

Written in the 14th Century

The glory of the world would be lost in oblivion if
God had not provided mortals with a remedy in books.
Towers are razed to the earth, cities are overthrown,
triumphal arches mouldered to dust; . . . as long as
the book exists the author cannot perish.

These are the masters who instruct us without rods
and ferrules, without hard words and anger, without
clothes or money. If you approach them, they are not
asleep; if investigating you interrogate them, they
conceal nothing; if you mistake them, they never
grumble; if you are ignorant, they never laugh at you.

In books we find the dead as it were living; in books
we foresee things to come; in books warlike affairs are
methodized; the rights of peace proceed from books.

Clarence Darrow, the Advocate, Always Free to Oppose

Excerpt from *Clarence Darrow for the Defense* by IRVING STONE

The one determination he made at this time was that he would remain unfettered. Nearly everybody in America belonged to something: a church, a political party, a fraternal order, an economic clique. He would belong to that rapidly diminishing brotherhood which owed allegiance to no man, creed or program. He feared set and rigid doctrine, no matter how valid it might look at the moment: its followers would too often oppose or close their eyes to change in the external world rather than be forced to make internal modifications. He knew that too often people accepted creeds, philosophies and panaceas because of their imperative need to believe in something, to belong to something, rather than because they had made a searching examination of its tenets and were intellectually convinced; that was why neither reasoning nor facts had much effect upon their emotional allegiances.

Since everyone around him was *for* something so passionately, he would remain free to be *against*. He would be Voltaire's "citizen of the world." It was not only that he saw the need in a swiftly changing society for the nonconformist, the detached critic, the astringent logician, but also that his nature and family heritage demanded this role of him.

"Darrow often debated and spoke for us socialists; he was a drawing card for the intellectuals. Yet we could never count him as one of us. He poked fun at us. He felt that no positive program could succeed in the face of an unpredictable future and lectured us on the need for a fluid program which would allow for modification."

He was in agreement with Kropotkin and the philosophical anarchists who claimed that the growth of government was a social evil because it curtailed the liberties of man and lent itself to manipulation by those interests which seized control; the seizing of the government by the railroads and the General Managers' Association during the A.R.U. strike was proof that the anarchists had a point. However, when he lectured to them or wrote articles for their press he always said: "I think you folks are right—but not altogether right. Your idea of free associations would have worked in a handicraft stage of society, like we had back in Kinsman when I was a boy, but you fail to take into account the growing machine age."

Before the freethinkers of America he committed the heresy of insisting that if they wished to remain freethinkers they had to make constant explorations into the realm of the spirit and that they had to build their freethinking on the hypothesis that they might be wrong. When the Atheists' Society invited him to lecture he dressed them down for being as arrogant and prejudiced as the church: religion insisted that there absolutely was a God, heaven and hell; the atheists insisted there absolutely was no God, no heaven and no hell, and neither could prove their point.

Since 1888 he had been attending the single-tax meetings and was considered one of its stanchest supporters, yet it had been his flailing of Henry George's speech that had won him his spurs—and the admiration of George and Mayor Cregier.

"One day Hamlin Garland lumbered in, threw himself into a roomy chair and from under his bushy eyebrows fixed his inquiring gaze on Clarence and asked, 'Well, Darrow, what's your latest slant?'

"Darrow crouched down into his coat collar, shrugged one shoulder higher than the other, peered across at Garland and said, 'That's what you always ask me.'

" 'Well, that's why I come here,' replied Garland, 'to get your latest slant on things. You know, you're one of the few who changes his mind with the times, and I'm always sure of hearing some new angle—how you've come to completely change your mind about one thing or other according to the turn of world affairs. You're the only man I know who hasn't the least pride — or shame — about admitting that he's been wrong; in fact, you kind of glory in pointing out that you've been fooled.'

" 'There's no such thing as standing still,' nodded Darrow. 'Unless a fellow moves ahead, he's left behind.' "

Proverbs to Ponder

The wisest man is he who regards others with mildness and himself with severity.

A bird in the hand is worth two in the bush.
A thousand cranes in the air are not worth one sparrow in the fist.

Birds of a feather flock together. Another version of—Show me your company and I'll tell you what you are.

Eat fire and your mouth will burn; live on credit and your pride will burn.

Fine feathers do not make fine birds.
Rich clothes cannot conceal a clown.

God bless those who pay visits—short ones.

He is wisest who holds his tongue.

Honesty is the best policy.

It never rains but it pours. (Seems to have been true all through the years.)

Knowledge begets humility; humility produces worthiness; worthiness encourages wealth; wealth sustains religion; and all together they create happiness.

Let wisdom and virtue be the two wheels of your cart.

Love me, love my dog.
"Who loves me, let him love my dog also."

Meditation should be done alone; study by two together; musical practice by three; traveling by four; agriculture by five; and battle by many.

A miss is as good as a mile. Allegedly from a naval engagement off Vera Cruz

One swallow does not make a summer. (Success must have durability to be truly noteworthy.)

Out of the frying pan into the fire. (From all ages, to describe the situation where the only retreat is something worse.)

The seat of knowledge is the head; of wisdom, the heart.

A slip of the tongue cuts deeper than the sword.

Spare the rod and spoil the child.

A stitch in time saves nine.

A teaspoonful of honey is worth a pound of gall. (A soft word turneth away wrath.)

Throw him into the river and he rises with a fish in his mouth. (Where another man would drown, the lucky man finds fish or pearls.)

Time drinks up the essence of great actions which should be quickly done but are delayed.

Too many cooks spoil the broth.
If the sailors become too numerous the ship sinks.

You can know ten things by learning one.

You cannot make a silk purse out of a sow's ear.

The walls have ears.

What is sown in the snow comes up in the thaw.

The wheel of fortune turns swifter than a mill wheel.
Good luck obtains a more rapid result than industry. So does bad luck.

Wisdom is one treasure no robber can touch.

The wise man inquires of himself the cause of his faults, the fool asks others.

The wise man ought to profit by all things—by the good and ills of life, the vices and virtues of others, by his own faults and his own good actions.

A Dream of Springtime

by EUGENE FIELD

I'm weary of this weather and I hanker for the ways
Which people read of in the psalms and preachers paraphrase—
The grassy fields, the leafy woods, the banks where I can lie
And listen to the music of the brook that flutters by,
Or, by the pond out yonder, hear the redwing blackbird's call
Where he makes believe he has a nest, but hasn't one at all;
And by my side should be a friend—a trusty, genial friend,
With plenteous store of tales galore and natural leaf to lend;
Oh, how I pine and hanker for the gracious boon of spring—
For *then* I'm going a-fishing with John Lyle King!

How like to pigmies will appear creation, as we float
Upon the bosom of the tide in a three-by-thirteen boat—
Forgotten all vexations and all vanities shall be,
As we cast our cares to windward and our anchor to the lee;

Anon the minnow-bucket will emit batrachian sobs,
And the devil's darning-needles shall come wooing of our bobs;
The sun shall kiss our noses and the breezes toss our hair
(This latter metaphoric—we've no fimbriae to spare!);
And I—transported by the bliss—shan't do a plaguey thing
But cut the bait and string the fish for John Lyle King!

Or, if I angle, it will be for bullheads and the like,
While he shall fish for gamey bass, for pickerel, and for pike;
I really do not care a rap for all the fish that swim—
But it's worth the wealth of Indies just to be along with him
In grassy fields, in leafy woods, beside the water-brooks,
And hear him tell of things he's seen or read of in his books—
To hear the sweet philosophy that trickles in and out
The while he is discoursing of the things we talk about;
A fountain-head refreshing—a clear, perennial spring
Is the genial conversation of John Lyle King!

Great Events from Little Causes

"In Roman history, it is found that the government was overthrown in consequence of Collatinus, praising his wife Lucretia. The love of Appius Claudius for Virginia destroyed the Decemvirate. The jealousy of a woman against her sister raised the Plebians to the consular dignity. Fulvia's disgust towards her lover caused the discovery of Cataline's conspiracy. Anthony and Octavius fought in consequence of the ugliness of Fulvia. The quarrel of two men of the lowest condition, the one a Genoese, the other a Venetian, occasioned a war between these republics, in which much wealth was expended and many valuable lives destroyed. A Genoese shoe maker caused the government of the republic to be changed. An empress treated her daughter with severity, and Attila in consequence ravaged Gaul and Italy, and laid the foundations of Venice. A game of dice settled the Vandals in Africa, and made them ravage Italy and sack Rome. Chilperic, king of France, struck his wife with a switch in sport and was assassinated in consequence. The settlement of the Lombards in Italy was occasioned by a repartee of the empress Sophia. Two Norman barons fought a duel, and thereby was established the kingdoms of Naples and Sicily. England and France were involved in bloody wars by the beauty of a young Turk. The khans of the Tartars and several cities were destroyed by the agency of a yellow goat. Francis I came near losing France by falling in love with a lady and promising to meet her at Lyons. Brittany was reunited to France, and England disturbed by civil commotions, by the love of the duchess dowager. A German struck a Genoese with a stick and caused the Austrians to be driven from the city, and Genoa recovered her liberty."

* * *

Hearts may agree, though heads may differ.

The Causes of War as Expressed in 1825

I N attempting a remedy for sickness, or any other evil, it is necessary first to investigate the cause. If that can be removed, a remedy may often be successfully applied. If it sometimes happens that past evils can only be deplored; it is certain, future evils can always be prevented, if we can prevent the cause.

The question "Whence come wars and fightings among you?" has been asked and answered in Holy Writ. Every war which has desolated the earth, may be traced to the "lust" of applause, power, gold, revenge, or some other lust equally vile; and we need only to look at the manifestos of belligerents to see, that they reciprocally charge each other with these motives.

The causes of war may be arranged under two general heads; viz. *ostensible* and *real.*

I shall endeavor to show that, even according to the declarations and avowals of the belligerents themselves, seven eighths of the wars, which have afflicted mankind, have had their orgin in *folly* and *wickedness;* and if we duly consider the *real* causes of wars, we shall find that at least nineteen twentieths have originated in *ambition* and *avarice.*

In considering the ostensible causes of war, I avail myself of the third report of the committee of inquiry instituted by the Massachusetts Peace Society. "In the report, the inquiry is confined to wars, in which civilized nations have been engaged, since they became christian, or since Constantine assumed the reins of the Roman empire: omitting a great number of petty wars, in small nations of antiquity, — temporary insurrections, or trivial hostilities — and a multitude of wars, which have been carried on between christian and savage nations, such as the aborigines of Asia and America. The report relates to 286 wars of magnitude, in which christian nations have been engaged. These are divided into the eleven following classes," viz: —

" 44 Wars of ambition to obtain extent of country.
22 Wars for plunder, tribute, &c.
24 Wars of retaliation or revenge.
8 Wars to settle some question of honor or prerogative.
6 Wars arising from disputed claims to some territory.
41 Wars arising from disputed titles to crowns.
30 Wars commenced under pretence of assisting an ally.
23 Wars originating in jealously of rival greatness.
5 Wars which have grown out of commerce.
55 Civil Wars.
28 Wars on account of religion, including the crusades against the Turks and heretics."

286

Holidays

by HENRY WADSWORTH LONGFELLOW
From *The Sonnets of Henry Wadsworth Longfellow*

The holiest of all holidays are those
  Kept by ourselves in silence and apart;
  The secret anniversaries of the heart,
  When the full river of feeling overflows;—
The happy days unclouded to their close;
  The sudden joys that out of darkness start
As flames from ashes; swift desires that dart
  Like swallows singing down each wind that blows!
White as the gleam of a receding sail,
  White as a cloud that floats and fades in air,
  White as the whitest lily on a stream,
These tender memories are;—a fairy tale
  Of some enchanted land we know not where,
  But lovely as a landscape in a dream.

Blessed Are the Happy-Hearted

Happiness is the sunshine of the heart. Its rays dispel the clouds in life's sky, and drive away tempests of doubt and storms of despair. If the heart is full of sunshine, it brims over in the eyes, and flows from the tongue like liquid silver. Happy words are ever welcome words, and blessed is he whose earthly mission is to make cheerful and bright those around him. There is always a corner in every household for the happy guest: the guest who is contented with everything, who demands little, and whose sunny presence is reflected in every face into which he looks. He has a courteous way of smoothing out little difficulties, and of smiling down impatient words, and of seeing the best side of everything. Blessed are the happy-hearted; would that earth had more of them!

> Do not look for wrong and evil,
>   You will find them if you do;
> As you measure for your neighbor
>   He will measure back to you.
>
> Look for goodness, look for gladness,
>   You will meet them all the while;
> If you bring a smiling visage
>   To the glass, you meet a smile.
>
> ALICE CARY

An effort made for the happiness of others lifts us above ourselves.— MRS. L. M. CHILD.

Surely happiness is reflective, . . . and every countenance bright with smiles, and glowing with innocent enjoyment, is a mirror transmitting to others the rays of a supreme and ever-shining benevolence.

> IRVING

THE STORY OF THE WHISTLE

by Benjamin Franklin

I received my dear friend's two letters, one for Wednesday and one for Saturday. This is again Wednesday. I do not deserve one for today, because I have not answered the former. But indolent as I am, and averse to writing, the fear of having no more of your pleasing epistles, if I do not contribute to the correspondence, obliges me to take up my pen: and as M. B. has kindly sent me word, that he sets out to-morrow to see you; instead of spending this Wednesday evening as I have long done its Name-sakes, in your delightful company, I sit down to spend it in thinking of you, in writing.to you, & in reading over and over again your letters.

I am charm'd with your description of Paradise, and with your plan of living there. And I approve much of your conclusion, that in the mean time we should draw all the good we can from this world. In my opinion we might all draw more good, from it than we do, and suffer less evil, if we would but take care *not to give too much for our Whistles.* For to me it seems that most of the unhappy people we meet with, are become so by neglect of that caution.

You ask what I mean?—You love stories, and will excuse my telling you one of my self. When I was a child of seven years old, my friends on a holiday fill'd my little pocket with halfpence. I went directly to a shop where they sold toys for children; and being charm'd with the sound of a whistle that I met by the way, in the hands of another boy, I voluntarily offer'd and gave all my money for it. When I came home, whistling all over the house, much pleas'd with my whistle, but disturbing all the family, my brothers, sisters & cousins, understanding the bargain I had made, told me I had given four times as much for it as it was worth, put me in mind what good things I might have bought with the rest of the money, & laught at me so much for my folly that I cry'd with vexation; and the reflection gave me more chagrin than the whistle gave me pleasure.

This however was afterwards of use to me, the impression continuing on my mind; so that often when I was tempted to buy some unnecessary thing, I said to my self, *Do not give too much for the Whistle;* and I sav'd my money.

As I grew up, came into the world, and observed the actions of men, I thought I met many *who gave too much for the Whistle.* — When I saw one ambitious of court favour, sacrificing

his time in attendance at levees, his repose, his liberty, his virtue and perhaps his friend, to obtain it; I have said to myself, *This man gives too much for his Whistle.* – When I saw another fond of popularity, constantly employing himself in political bustles; neglecting his own affairs, and ruining them by that neglect, *He pays*, says I, *too much for his Whistle.* – If I knew a miser, who gave up every kind of comfortable living, all the pleasure of doing good to others, all the esteem of his fellow citizens, & the joys of benevolent friendship, for the sake of accumulating wealth, *Poor Man*, says I, *you pay too much for your Whistle.* – When I met with a man of pleasure, sacrificing every laudable improvement of his mind or of his fortune, to mere corporeal satisfactions, & ruining his health in their pursuit, *Mistaken Man*, says I, *you are providing pain for yourself instead of pleasure, you pay too much for your Whistle.* – If I see one fond of appearance, of fine cloaths, fine houses, fine furniture, fine equipages, all above his fortune, for which he contracts debts, and ends his career in a prison; *Alas*, says I, *he has paid too much for his Whistle.* – When I saw a beautiful sweet-temper'd girl, marry'd to an ill-natured brute of a husband; *What a pity*, says I, *that she should pay so much for a Whistle!* – In short, I conceiv'd that great part of the miseries of mankind, were brought upon them by the false estimates they had made of the value of things, and by their *giving too much for the Whistle.*

Yet I ought to have charity for these unhappy people, when I consider that with all this wisdom of which I am boasting, there are certain things in the world so tempting; for example the apples of King John, which happily are not to be bought, for if they were put to sale by auction, I might very easily be led to ruin my self in the purchase, and find that I had once more *given too much for the Whistle.*

Adieu, my dearest friend, and believe me ever yours very sincerely and with unalterable affection.

No More "Might-Have-Beens"

The great world-clock of Time still keeps its beat.
NATHANIEL HAWTHORNE

Do you realize how fast time is flying? We have buried our Winter, and now our Spring-tide is fast drifting out, and still time flies on. Look back over the days of the year. How much you have to be sorry for—how much to be glad for! When you walk out in the evening under the street lamps, what myriads of little insects you see flying around in the circle of the light! These are like the clustering little regrets that hover about you wherever you go; things that make you sorry, and fill you with longings for lost opportunities,— the sad "might have beens" of the year. Oh, for a chance to go back and redeem yourself! — this is your cry; yet why grieve over it now? Improve the present, lest it, too, rise up to haunt you in coming days.

Who looking backward from his manhood's prime,
Sees not the spectre of his misspent time?
JOHN GREENLEAF WHITTIER

Oh, the wasted hours of life
  That have drifted by;
Oh, the good we might have done,
  Lost without a sigh;
Love that we might once have saved
  By a single word;
Thoughts conceived, but never penned,
  Perishing unheard.
ANONYMOUS

Duty and To-day are ours: results and futurity belong to God.
HORACE GREELEY

Sir, Said Dr. Johnson

Sir, when a man is invited to dinner he is disappointed if he does not get something good.

Any of us would kill a cow rather than not have beef.

A man seldom thinks with more earnestness of anything than he does of his dinner.

Some people have a foolish way of not minding, or of pretending not to mind, what they eat. For my part I mind my belly very studiously and very carefully for I look upon it that he who does not mind his belly will hardly mind anything else.

Sir, I do not say it is wrong to produce self-complacency by drinking; I only deny that it improves the mind.

Sir, claret is the liquor for boys, port for men, but he who aspires to be a hero must drink brandy.

There are some sluggish men who are improved by drinking, as there are fruits which are not good till they are rotten.

★   ★   ★

There is no sauce like Appetite.

Cheese and Ham are good companions.

Bread and cheese make a healthy man.

Between the hand and the mouth the soup is often lost.

Castor and Polydeukes (Pollux)

The true test of brotherhood

Since Castor and his brother Polydeukes came long ago as guests to the house of Pamphaes, no marvel is it that Pamphaes's sons are mightly athletes born; for these two, guardian-gods of spacious Sparta, preside with Hermes and Hercules over the blooming lot of the contests, making men of upright life their special charge; for faithful in very truth is the race of gods.

In turn they spend their days, one day together they enjoy with Zeus, their father, and one day they spend beneath the dark earth in the dells of Therapne, thus fulfilling an equal fate. For Polydeukes made the choice for them, when Castor died in war, rather than to be himself altogether an immortal and dwell in heaven. For Idas angered about his herd, slew Castor with his brazen spear after Lynceus, whose of all men's was the piercing eye, had beheld the brothers lurking in the shade of an ancient oak. So hastening with nimble feet, Idas and Lynceus came and quickly wrought the bold deed for which they suffered at the hands of Zeus a grievous retribution. Forthwith the other son of Leda came in hot pursuit, and these opposing him took stand hard by their father's tomb, from whence they snatched a polished stone, decoration of death, and hurled it at the breast of Polydeukes; but they crushed him not, nor drove him back; for rushing on with spear swift in motion, he drove the pointed brass into the side of Lynceus, while Zeus upon Idas hurled his smouldering thunderbolt, and both were burned together, reft of mourners; for men intermeddle not in a contest with the mighty ones.

Speedily to his brother returned the mighty son of Zeus, and found him not yet dead, but with short-drawn breath, gasping forth his life. Then shedding warm tears with sobs, he cried loud and clear: "O Father, son of Cronos, what end shall ever be of these my sorrows? To me also with him ordain strong death, O King. Honor is gone from man bereft of friends; and in distress few mortals be faithful enough to share his labor."

Thus then he prayed, and Zeus before him came and spoke:—
"Thou art my son, but he the later born of mortal seed;
yet come, of this in truth I give thee choice; if thou art willing
to escape death and hateful age and in Olympus dwell with
Athene and Ares of the bloody spear, this is thy rightful lot;
but if for thy brother's sake thou pleadest, and art mindful
to share with him an equal part of all thou hast, then half
thy life thou must spend beneath the earth, half in the golden
homes of heaven."

When thus he spake, no wavering resolution did the mind
of Polydeukes hold; so Zeus unclosed the eyes, and loosed the
voice of Castor the brazen-belted.

Pindar

Our Oldest Friend

by OLIVER WENDELL HOLMES

I give you the health of the oldest friend
That, short of eternity, earth can lend,—
A friend so faithful and tried and true
That nothing can wean him from me and you.

When first we screeched in the sudden blaze
Of the daylight's blinding and lasting rays,
And gulped at the gaseous, groggy air,
This old, old friend stood waiting there.

And when, with a kind of mortal strife,
We had gasped and choked into breathing life,
He watched by the cradle, day and night,
And held our hands till we stood upright.

From gristle and pulp our frames have grown
To stringy muscle and solid bone;
While we were changing, he altered not;
We might forget, but he never forgot.

He came with us in the college class,—
Little cared he for the steward's pass!
All the rest must pay their fee,
But the grim old deadhead entered free.

He stayed with us while we counted o'er
Four tunes each of the seasons four;
And with every season from year to year,
The dear name Classmate he made more dear.

He never leaves us,— he never will,
Till our hands are cold and our hearts are still.
On birthdays, and Christmas, and New Years too,
He always remembers both me and you.

Every year this faithful friend
His little presents is sure to send;
Every year, wheresoe'er we be,
He wants a keepsake from you and me.

How he loves us! he pats our heads,
And, lo! they are gleaming with silver threads;
And he's always begging one lock of hair
Till our shining crowns have nothing to wear.

At length he will tell us, one by one,
"My child, your labor on earth is done;
And now you must journey afar to see
My elder brother,— Eternity!"

And so, when long, long years have passed,
Some dear old fellow will be the last,—
Never a boy alive but he
Of all our goodly company!

When he lies down, but not till then,
Our kind Class-Angel will drop the pen
That writes in the day-book kept above
Our lifelong record of faith and love.

So here's a health in homely rhyme
To our oldest Classmate, Father Time!
May our last survivor live to be
As bald and as wise and as tough as he!

Don Quixote and Sancho Panza

A story of the perfect optimist

"Sancho," said Don Quixote, "let us lay aside all manner of animosity; let us forget and forgive injuries; and answer me as speedily as thou canst, without any remains of thy last displeasure, how, when, and where didst thou find my lady Dulcinea? What was she doing when thou first paid'st thy respects to her? How didst thou express thyself to her? What answer was she pleased to make thee? What countenance did she put on at the perusal of my letter? Who transcribed it fairly for thee? And everything else which has any relation to this affair, without addition, lies, or flattery. On the other side, take care thou losest not a tittle of the whole matter, by abbreviating it, lest thou rob me of part of that delight, which I propose to myself from it."— "Sir," answered Sancho, "if I must speak the truth, and nothing but the truth, nobody copied out the letter for me; for I carried none at all."—"That's right," cried Don Quixote, "for I found the pocket-book, in which it was written, two days after thy departure, which occasioned exceeding grief in me, because I knew not what thou could'st do, when thou found'st thyself without the letter; and I could not but be induced to believe that thou would'st have returned, in order to take it with thee."— "I had certainly done so," replied Sancho, "were it not for this head of mine, which kept it in remembrance ever since your worship read it to me, and helped me to say it over to a parish-clerk, who writ it out for me word for word so purely, that he swore, though he had written out many a letter of excommunication in his time, he never in all the days of his life had read or seen anything so well spoken as it was."—"And dost thou still retain the memory of it, my dear Sancho?" cried Don Quixote.—"Not I," quoth Sancho; "for as soon as I had given it her, and your turn was served, I was very willing to forget it. But if I remember anything, it is what was on the top; and it was thus: High and superficial, I would say, sovereign lady; and at the bottom, Yours until death, the Knight of the Doleful Countenance; and I put between these two things three hundred souls and lives and pigsnyes."

"All this is mighty well," said Don Quixote; "proceed, therefore: you arrived, and how was that queen of beauty then employed? On my conscience, thou found'st her stringing of orient pearls, or embroidering some curious device in gold for me her captive knight; was it not so, my Sancho?"—"No, faith," answered the squire, "I found her winnowing a parcel of wheat very seriously in the back yard."—"Then," said the Don, "you may rest assured that every corn of that wheat was a grain of pearl,

since she did it the honor of touching it with her divine hand.
Didst thou observe the quality of the wheat, was it not of the
finest sort?"—"Very indifferent, I thought," said the squire.—
"Well, this, at least, you must allow; it must make the finest
whitest bread, if sifted by her white hands. But go on; when you
delivered my letter, did she kiss it? Did she treasure it in her
bosom, or what ceremony did she use worthy such a letter? How
did she behave herself?"—"Why, truly, sir," answered Sancho,
"when I offered her the letter, she was very busy handling her
sieve; 'and, pr'ythee, honest friend,' said she, 'do so much as lay
that letter down upon that sack there; I cannot read it till I have
winnowed out what is in my hands.' "—"O unparalleled discre-
tion!" cried Don Quixote; "she knew that a perusal required
leisure, and therefore deferred it, for her more pleasing and
private hours. But oh! my squire, while she was thus employed,
what conference passed? What did she ask about her knight, and
what did you reply? Say all, say all, my dearest Sancho, let not
the smallest circumstance scape the tongue; speak all that thought

can frame, or pen describe."—"Her questions were easily answered, sir," said Sancho, "for she asked me none at all: I told her, indeed, in what a sad pickle I had left you for her sake, naked to the waist; that you ate and slept like the brute beasts; that you would let a razor as soon touch your throat as your beard; that you were still blubbering and crying, or swearing and cursing your fortune."—"There you mistook," replied Don Quixote. "I rather bless my fortune, and always shall, while life affords me breath, since I am thought to merit the esteem of so high a lady as Dulcinea del Toboso."—"There you hit it," said Sancho; "she is a high lady, indeed, sir, for she is taller than I am by half a foot."—"Why, how now, Sancho," said the knight, "hast thou measured with her?"—"Ah, marry did I, sir," said the squire; "for you must know that she desired me to lend her a hand in lifting a sack of wheat on an ass; so we buckled about it, and I came so close to her, that I found she was taller than I by a full span at least."—"Right," answered Don Quixote; "but thou art also conscious that the uncommon stature of her person is adorned with innumerable graces and endowments of soul. But, Sancho, when you approached near to her did not an aromatic smell strike thy sense, a scent so odoriferous, pleasing, and sweet, that I want a name for it; sweet as — you understand me, as the richest fragrancy diffused around a perfumer's magazine of odors? This, at least, you must grant me."—"I did indeed feel a sort of scent a little unsavory," said Sancho, "somewhat vigorous or so; for I suppose she had wrought hard, and sweated somewhat."—"It is false," answered the knight, "thy smelling has been debauched by thy own scent, or some canker in thy nose: if thou could'st tell the scent of opening roses, fragrant lilies, or the choicest amber, then thou might'st guess at hers."— "Cry mercy, sir," said Sancho; "it may be so indeed, for I remember that I myself have smelt very oft just as Madam Dulcinea did then; and it is no such wondrous thing neither that one devil should be like another."

"But now," said the knight, "supposing the corn winnowed and despatched to the mill, what did she after she had read my letter?"—"Your letter, sir," answered Sancho, "your letter was not read at all, sir; as for her part, she said, she could neither read nor write, and she would trust nobody else, lest they should tell tales, and so she cunningly tore your letter. She said, that what I told her by word of mouth of your love and penance was enough: to make short now, she gave her service to you, and said she had rather see you than hear from you; and she prayed you, if ever you loved her, upon sight of me, forthwith to leave your madness among the bushes here, and come straight to Toboso (if you be at leisure), for she has something to say to you, and has a huge mind to see you: she had like to burst with laughing, when I called you the Knight of the Doleful Countenance. She told me the Biscayan whom you mauled so was there, and that he was a very honest fellow; but that she heard no news at all of the galley-slaves."

"Thus far all goes well," said Don Quixote; "but tell me, pray, what jewel did she present you at your departure, as a reward for the news you brought? for it is a custom of ancient standing among knights and ladies errant, to bestow on squires, dwarfs, or damsels, who bring them good news of their ladies or servants, some precious jewel as a grateful reward of their welcome tidings."

—"Ah! sir," said Sancho, "that was the fashion in the days of yore, and a very good fashion, I take it: but all the jewels Sancho got was a luncheon of bread and a piece of cheese, which she handed to me over the wall, when I was taking my leave, by the same token (I hope there's no ill luck in it), the cheese was made of sheep's milk."—"It is strange," said Don Quixote, "for she is liberal, even to profuseness; and if she presented thee not a jewel, she had certainly none about her at that time; but what is deferred is not lost, sleeves are good after Easter. I shall see her, and matters shall be accommodated."

Cervantes

TO-MORROW

From: *The Sonnets of Henry Wadsworth Longfellow*
arranged with an introduction by Ferris Greenslet
Copyright Houghton Mifflin & Company 1907

'Tis late at night, and in the realm of sleep
  My little lambs are folded like the flocks;
  From room to room I hear the wakeful clocks
  Challenge the passing hour, like guards that keep
Their solitary watch on tower and steep;
  Far off I hear the crowing of the cocks,
  And through the opening door that time unlocks
  Feel the fresh breathing of To-morrow creep.
To-morrow! the mysterious, unknown guest,
  Who cries to me: "Remember Barmecide,
  And tremble to be happy with the rest."
And I make answer: "I am satisfied;
  I dare not ask; I know not what is best;
  God hath already said what shall betide."

· 49 ·

We Once Were Children

by HEINRICH HEINE

My child, we once were children,
  Two children, little and gay;
We crawl'd inside the henhouse,
  And hid in the straw in play.

We crow'd as the cocks are accustom'd,
  And when the people came by,
"Cock-a-doodle-doo!"— and they fancied
  'Twas really the cock's shrill cry.

The chests within our courtyard
  With paper we nicely lined,
And in them lived together,
  In a dwelling quite to our mind.

The aged cat of our neighbor
  Came oft to visit us there;
We made her our bows and our curtsies,
  And plenty of compliments fair.

For her health we used to inquire
  In language friendly and soft;
Since then we have ask'd the same question
  Of many old cats full oft.

We used to sit, while we wisely
  Discoursed, in the way of old men,
And lamented that all was better
  In the olden days than then;

How love and truth and religion
From out of the world had fled,
How very dear was the coffee,
How scarce was the gold, we said.

Those childish sports have vanish'd,
And all is fast rolling away;
The world, and the times, and religion,
And gold, love, and truth all decay.

Ode: Intimations of Immortality

From *Recollections of Early Childhood*
by WILLIAM WORDSWORTH

The Fifth Stanza

Our birth is but a sleep and a forgetting:
The Soul that rises with us, our life's star,
    Hath had elsewhere its setting,
    And cometh from afar:
    Not in entire forgetfulness,
    And not in utter nakedness,
But trailing clouds of glory do we come
    From God, who is our home:
Heaven lies about us in our infancy!
Shades of the prison-house begin to close
    Upon the growing Boy,
But he beholds the light, and whence it flows,
    He sees it in his joy;
The Youth, who daily farther from the east
    Must travel, still is Nature's Priest,
    And by the vision splendid
    Is on his way attended;
At length the Man perceives it die away,
And fade into the light of common day.

"Live As Your Wise Forefathers Lived Before You"...words of Chief Pontiac to his people

by Edwin D. Wood, LL.D.; From *Historic Mackinac*

"A 'Delaware Indian,' said Pontiac, 'conceived an eager desire to learn wisdom from the Master of Life; but, being ignorant where to find him, he had recourse to fasting, dreaming, and magical incantations. By these means it was revealed to him, that, by moving forward in a straight, undeviating course, he would reach the abode of the Great Spirit. He told his purpose to no one, and having provided the equipments of a hunter —gun, powder-horn, ammunition, and a kettle for preparing his food,—he set out on his errand. For some time he journeyed on in high hope and confidence.

On the evening of the eighth day, he stopped by the side of a brook at the edge of a meadow, where he began to make ready his evening meal, when, looking up, he saw three large openings in the woods before him, and three well-beaten paths which entered them. He was much surprised; but his wonder increased, when, after it had grown dark, the three paths were more clearly visible than ever. Remembering the important object of his journey, he could neither rest nor sleep; and, leaving his fire, he crossed the meadow, and entered the largest of the three openings. He had advanced but a short distance into the forest, when a bright flame sprang out of the ground before him, and arrested his steps.

In great amazement, he turned back, and entered the second path, where the same wonderful phenomenon again encountered him; and now, in terror and bewilderment, yet still resolved to persevere, he took the last of the three paths. On this he journeyed a whole day without interruption, when, at length, emerging from the forest, he saw before him a vast mountain, of dazzling whiteness. So precipitous was the ascent that the Indian thought it hopeless to go farther, and looked around him in despair: at that moment, he saw, seated at some distance above, the figure of a beautiful woman arrayed in white, who arose as he looked upon her, and thus accosted him: 'How can you hope, encumbered as you are, to succeed in your design? Go down to the foot of the mountain, throw away your gun, your ammunition, your provisions, and your clothing; wash yourself in the stream which flows there, and

you will then be prepared to stand before the Master of Life.'
The Indian obeyed, and again began to ascend among the
rocks, while the woman, seeing him still discouraged, laughed
at his faintness of heart, and told him that, if he wished for
success, he must climb by the aid of one hand and one foot only.

After great toil and suffering, he at length found himself at
the summit. The woman had disappeared, and he was left
alone. A high and beautiful plain lay before him, and at a little
distance he saw three great villages, far superior to the squalid
wigwams of the Delawares. As he approached the largest, and
stood hesitating whether he should enter, a man gorgeously
attired stepped forth, and, taking him by the hand, welcomed
him to the celestial abode. He then conducted him to the presence of the Great Spirit, where the Indian stood confounded
by the unspeakable splendour which surrounded him. The
Great Spirit bade him be seated, and thus addressed him: —

"'I am the Maker of heaven and earth, the trees, lakes, rivers, and all things else. I am the Maker of Mankind; and because I love you, you must do my will. The land on which you
live I have made for you, and not for others. Why do you suffer the white men to dwell among you? My children, you have
forgotten the customs and traditions of your forefathers. Why

do you not clothe yourselves in skins as they did, and use the bows and arrows, and the stone-painted lances, which they used? You have bought guns, knives, kettles, and blankets, from the white men, until you can no longer do without them; and, what is worse, you have drunk the poison fire-water, which turns you into fools. Fling all these things away; live as your wise forefathers lived before you. And as for these English,—these dogs dressed in red, who have come to rob you of your hunting-grounds, and drive away the game,—you must lift the hatchet against them. Wipe them from the face of the earth, and then you will win my favour back again, and once more be happy and prosperous."

Such was Pontiac's tale to the assembled Indians as told by Parkman, the eminent historian and author.

THE WANTS OF MAN

by JOHN QUINCY ADAMS

"Man wants but little here below,
Nor wants that little long."
'Tis not with me exactly so—
But 'tis so in the song.
My wants are many, and, if told,
Would muster many a score;
And were each wish a mint of gold,
I still should long for more.

What first I want is daily bread,
And canvas-backs and wine;
And all the realms of Nature spread
Before me when I dine.
Four courses scarcely can provide
My appetite to quell,
With four choice cooks from France beside,
To dress my dinner well.

What next I want, at heavy cost,
Is elegant attire;
Black sable furs for winter's frost,
And silks for summer's fire,
And Cashmere shawls, and Brussels lace,
My bosom's front to deck,
And diamond rings my hands to grace,
And rubies for my neck.

And then I want a mansion fair,
A dwelling house, in style;
Four stories high, for wholesome air—
A massive marble pile;
With halls for banquets and for balls;
All furnish'd rich and fine;
With stabled steeds in fifty stalls,
And cellars for my wine.

I want a garden and a park
My dwelling to surround,
A thousand acres (bless the mark!),
With walls encompass'd round,
Where flocks may range and herds may low,
And kids and lambkins play;
And flowers and fruits commingled grow,
All Eden to display.

I want, when summer's foliage falls,
And autumn strips the trees,
A house within the city's walls
For comfort and for ease—
But here, as space is somewhat scant,
And acres somewhat rare,
My house in town I only want
To occupy—a Square.

Woodman, Spare That Tree

by GEORGE POPE MORRIS

Woodman, spare that tree!
 Touch not a single bough!
In youth it sheltered me,
 And I'll protect it now.
'Twas my forefather's hand
 That placed it near his cot;
There, woodman, let it stand—
 Thy axe shall harm it not!

That old familiar tree,
 Whose glory and renown
Are spread o'er land and sea—
 And wouldst thou hew it down?
Woodman, forbear thy stroke!
 Cut not its earth-bound ties;
Oh, spare that aged oak,
 Now towering to the skies!

When but an idle boy,
   I sought its grateful shade;
In all their gushing joy
   Here, too, my sisters played.
My mother kissed me here;
   My father pressed my hand—
Forgive this foolish tear,
   But let that old oak stand!

My heart-strings round thee cling,
   Close as thy bark, old friend!
Here shall the wild-bird sing,
   And still thy branches bend.
Old tree! the storm still brave!
   And, woodman, leave the spot;
While I've a hand to save,
   Thy axe shall harm it not!

FROM QUIP TO ZIP

In these days of conversion to the Zip Code to automate the postal system, the fun and informality of the early postal service can be appreciated by all.

The exterior, as well as the interior of a letter was sometimes made the vehicle of sentiment, affection, wit, fun, and the like, which, thus riding as outside passengers, displayed their beauties to the gaze of those connected with post offices. In such instances it may have been that the writer's ideas, gushing from his pen, overflowed their bounds, and spread themselves upon the usually dry surface of the epistle. It must have been a pleasing relief to post office clerks, wearied with the monotonous task of turning up innumerable names, to find the flowers of fancy and imagination supplanting the endless catalogue of Smiths and Browns which ordinarily met their eyes. Below are a few specimens of these embellished addresses.

OUTSIDE RHYMES

All flesh is grass: all paper's rags,
(So it is said by wicked wags.)
But I would like to pass along
Among th' epistolary throng,
Till I reach the town of Kent
Nor to a paper mill be sent,
And come to an untimely end,
Before I find my writer's friend;
Whose name is Putnam, or Sam Put,
In the old State Connecticut.

* * *

This is going to my tailor,
A *trust*-worthy man is he;
Like a clock, for ever *ticking*,
He keeps his account with me.

To send my bill I here request him
For the br—ches he has made:
Thanks to good old uncle Samuel,
He must send it on *pre-paid*.
(The address was in prose.)

* * *

When you C this letter,
You'd better letter B.
For it is going over
Unto Tom McG.
In the town of Dover,
State of Tennessee.

* * *

I want this letter to go right straight
To Wilmington city in Delaware State,
To Daniel B. Woodard, a cooper by trade;
He can make as good barrels as ever were made.

* * *

Swiftly hasten, Postman's organ,
  Bear this onward to its fate,
In New York to George C. Morgan;
  John Street, No. 78

* * *

East 10th Street, City of New York,
  Two hundred fifty-three—
Is where of all this little work,
  This moment ought to be

And could I to the lightning's wing
  Or telegraphic wire,
Attach it by a silken string,
  'Twould be my fond desire.

But since to do the swift exploit
  Each other power must fail,
I send to Emily Bailey Hoyt,
  With pleasure—in the mail.

* * *

I know a man, his name is Dunn!
  He lives in splendid style:
But if he'd pay—say half his debts,
  He'd lose 'bout all his *"pile."*

* * *

He stops in Charlestown, old Bay State,
  Quite near to Bunker Hill,
Where many a brave man met his fate,
  Dispensing Putnam Pill.

ADDRESSES ON VALENTINES

Lizzie, they say the little birds
  Are making matches now;
(Warranted to keep in any climate.)
A good example they have set
  Which I would like to follow;
So if you have a heart to let,
  I hope to know to-morrow.

* * *

Mr. Post Master, keep this well,
for every line is going to tell
how much I love my Bill Martell,
Syracuse, N. Y.

· 59 ·

ODD SUPERSCRIPTIONS

To Mr Leedfara, who runs the ferry
over across to Long Island for Mary
Maguire New York.

* * *

Mistress Crovor Keeps
a stand in the
hutson dippo—New York
lives in reed street.

* * *

Direct this letter to
315 Second floor
Back room for Kate
Barrey washington street
New York
in heast.

* * *

To the Lady that wears a white cloak Straw
Bonnett trimmed with Blue & wears a blue
veil, brown or striped dress
No—Bleeker street
New York.

* * *

To Don Tom Rigan
and Monseer Birch—
To New York city straight let this 'ere letter go
Right to der corner of der Bowery and Grand
Into Jim Story's place which every one must know
Onto I forgot his name's old oyester stand.
The *blades* it's intended for are hearty and frisky,
You'll find backe of der bar, where yer give dis letter.
The postman may find himself a cocktail der better.

* * *

P. O. No 9 Albany Street
Boston State of Mass for Michael
Ryan tailor and if he do not
live here i expect that the
Person who will live here will
forward this letter to him
if they chance to know
where he live.

* * *

Sailing Down the Ohio

by JOHN JAMES AUDUBON, noted naturalist and painter
Written about 1830

THE natural features of North America are not less remarkable than the moral character of her inhabitants, and I cannot find a better subject than one of those magnificent rivers that roll the collected waters of her extensive territories to the ocean.

When my wife, my eldest son, (then an infant,) and myself, were returning from Pennsylvania to Kentucky, we found it expedient, the waters being unusually low, to provide ourselves with a *skiff*, to enable us to proceed to our abode at Henderson. I purchased a large, commodious vessel of that denomination. We procured a matress, and our friends furnished us with ready prepared viands. We had two stout negro rowers, and in this trim we left the village of Shippingport, in expectation of reaching the place of our destination in a very few days.

It was in the month of October. The autumnal tints already decorated the shores of that queen of rivers, the Ohio. Every tree was hung with long and flowing festoons of different species of vines, many loaded with clustered fruits of varied brilliancy, their rich bronzed carmine mingling beautifully with the yellow foliage, which now predominated over the yet green leaves reflecting more lively tints from the clear stream than ever landscape painter pourtrayed, or poet imagined.

The days were yet warm. The sun had assumed the rich and glowing hue which at that season produces the singular phenomenon called there the "Indian summer." The moon had rather passed the meridian of her grandeur. We glided down the river, meeting no other ripple of the water than that formed by the propulsion of our boat. Leisurely we moved along, gazing all day on the grandeur and beauty of the wild scenery around us.

Now and then a large cat-fish rose to the surface of the water in pursuit of a shoal or fry, which, starting simultaneously from the liquid element, like so many silvery arrows, produced a shower of light, while the pursuer with open jaws seized the stragglers, and with a splash of his tail, disappeared from our view. Other fishes we heard uttering beneath our bark a rumbling noise, the strange sounds of which we discovered to proceed from the white perch, for on casting our net from the bow, we caught several of that species, when the noise ceased for some time.

John James Audubon, American naturalist and artist —
from an engraving after an original painting by Chappel

Nature, in her varied arrangements, seems to have felt a partiality towards this portion of our country. As the traveller ascends or descends the Ohio, he cannot help remarking, that alternately, nearly the whole length of the river, the margin, on one side, is bounded by lofty hills and a rolling surface; while, on the other, extensive plains of the richest alluvial land are seen as far as the eye can command the view. Islands of varied size and form rise here and there from the bosom of the water, and the winding course of the stream frequently brings you to places where the idea of being on a river of great length changes to that of floating on a lake of moderate extent. Some of these islands are of considerable size and value; while others, small and insignificant, seem as if intended for contrast, and as serving to enhance the general interest of the scenery. These little islands are frequently overflowed during great *freshets* or floods, and receive at their heads prodigious heaps of drifted timber. We foresaw with great concern the alterations that cultivation would soon produce along those delightful banks.

As night came, sinking in darkness the broader portions of the river, our minds became affected by strong emotions, and wandered far beyond the present moments. The tinkling of bells told us that the cattle which bore them were gently roving from valley to valley in search of food, or retiring to their distant homes. The hooting of the great owl, or the muffled noise of its wings as it sailed smoothly over the stream were matters of interest to us; so was the sound of the boatman's horn, as it came winding more and more softly from afar. When daylight returned, many songsters burst forth with echoing notes, more and more mellow to the listening ear. Here and there the lonely cabin of a squatter struck the eye, giving note of commencing civilization. The crossing of the stream by a deer foretold how soon the hill would be covered with snow.

A Boy's Song

by JAMES HOGG

Where the pools are bright and deep,
Where the grey trout lies asleep,
Up the river and over the lea,
That's the way for Billy and me.

Where the blackbird sings the latest,
Where the hawthorn blooms the sweetest,
Where the nestlings chirp and flee,
That's the way for Billy and me.

Where the mowers mow the cleanest,
Where the hay lies thick and greenest,
There to track the homeward bee,
That's the way for Billy and me.

Where the hazel bank is steepest,
Where the shadow falls the deepest,
Where the clustering nuts fall free,
That's the way for Billy and me.

Why the boys should drive away
Little sweet maidens from the play,
Or love to banter and fight so well,
That's the thing I never could tell.

But this I know, I love to play
Through the meadow, among the hay;
Up the water and over the lea,
That's the way for Billy and me.

Make a Person Happy

Don't wait to say the needed word, or to do the needed kindness. Life, at the longest, is only a brief span; therefore don't let its chances pass you by. Give not only the kind and friendly word, but the encouraging and helpful one, as well. Commendation, when it is deserved, will make many a burden lighter.

A word—and the skies would brighten;
    A word—and the clouds would fly;
A word—and the soul find healing,
    And hurt hearts cease to sigh.

Oh, word ere too late, be spoken!
    Let the threshold of silence be crossed,
Ere the thread of thy fate be broken
    And thy chance forever be lost!

MARK F. GRISWOLD

· 65 ·

The Road to Success

From *The Tennessee Farmer, 1834*

To constitute an accomplished farmer, one who can pursue the honorable occupation to which he belongs, with honor, with profit, and with pleasure to himself, and with advantage to his country, the following traits of character are almost indispensable.

1. He must be a man of integrity — one who would scorn to defraud his land, his beasts, his servants, or his neighbors — because, by doing either, he always injures himself, and often injures his country.

2. He must be a man of thought and reflection — for without these he can never know how to direct his industry, or understanding in what economy consists — and without well directed industry, and a wise and prudent economy, no farmer can prosper.

3. He must understand how to create and how to preserve the fertility of his land — because, without increasing and preserving the fertility of his soil, his labor will generally prove to be both unprofitable to himself and injurious to his country.

4. He must know how to cultivate his land in that manner which will enable him to obtain the largest product it is capable of yielding with least expense.

5. He must understand the best mode of rearing stock, and improving their breed.

6. He must have industry enough to reduce his knowledge to practice — otherwise it can be of no value either to himself or to his country.

7. He must well understand the distinction between true and false economy, and rigidly practice the former, and avoid the latter — otherwise his labor will only be thrown away.

8. He must be too wise to be vain and self-conceited — otherwise he will be above improving in his profession — and besides vanity and self-conceit are disgusting and odious to others, and the most certain and infallible proofs of a weakened intellect and a corrupt heart.

9. He must possess a benevolent temper and disposition — because, without this, he can never so use the product of his last labors, as either to promote his own or the happiness of others.

10. He must be patriotic. This will induce him to seek to promote the public good, in which his own interest is involved.

11. He must have too much honorable independence of soul to be capable of degrading himself into a slavish partisan — otherwise he will infallibly become the dupe of artful and intriguing demagogues, or of corrupt political aspirants, who will be sure to use him for the accomplishment of their own base purposes, to the great injury of himself and of his country.

12. And to crown all, he should be a man of real genuine piety—a piety that will prompt him in whatever he may be engaged, whether in the labors of the field, in the duties pertaining to social intercourse, or in those of devotion.

The Rules of Good Business Practice in 1850

1. Endeavor to be perfect in the calling you are engaged in; and be assiduous in every part thereof:—*Industry* being the natural means of acquiring *wealth, honor,* and *reputation.*

2. Lay a good foundation in regard to principle. Be sure not willfully to overreach or deceive your neighbor; but keep always in your eye the golden rule of *Doing as you would be done by.*

3. Be strict in discharging all legal debts. Do not evade your creditors by any shuffling arts, in giving notes under your hand, only to defer payment; but if you have it in your power, discharge all debts when they become due. Above all, when you are straitened for want of money, be cautious of taking it up at high interest. This has been the ruin of many; therefore endeavor to avoid it.

4. Endeavor to be as much in your shop or warehouse, or in whatever place your business properly lies, as you possibly can. Leave it not to servants to transact; for customers will not regard them.

5. Be complaisant to the *meanest* as well as to the *greatest.* You are as much obliged to use good manners for a farthing as a pound; the one demands it from you as well as the other.

6. Be not too talkative, but speak as much as is necessary to recommend your goods, and always observe to keep within the rules of decency, and truth.

7. Take great care in keeping your accounts well. Enter every-thing necessary in your books with neatness and exactness; often state your accounts, and examine whether you gain or lose, and carefully survey your stock, and inspect every particular of your affairs.

8. Take care, as much as you can, whom you trust. Neither *take* nor *give long credit;* but at the farthest, annually settle your accounts. Deal, if it lies in your power, for ready money. This method you will find to be most profitable in the end. Endeavor to keep a proper assortment in your way, but not overstock yourself. Make your *business* your pleas-ure, and other entertainments will appear necessary only for relaxation from it.

9. Strive to maintain a *fair character* in the world; that will be the best means for advancing your credit, gaining you the most flourishing trade, and enlarging your fortune. Con-descend to no *mean* action, but add a luster to trade by keeping up to the principles of justice and Christian morality.

* * *

HOW TO MAKE LIFE MORE PLEASANT

by BALTHASAR GRACIAN

Have friends.—It is the second existence. Every friend is good and wise for his friend, and among them all gets well managed. . . .

Be common in nothing, above all not in taste. . . .

Never open the door to an evil, however small, for other and greater ones will creep in after it from their ambush. . . .

Think with the few, and speak with the many.

Overcome your antipathies.

Be able to wait.— . . . First be master of yourself if you would be master of others. Only through the spaces of time do we come to the centre of opportunity. . . . He spake a great word who said, Time and I against any two.

Understand the art of refusing.— . . . The No of some people is more esteemed than the Yes of others, for a gilded No satis-fies more than a dry Yes. . . .

Do not be unsociable.—In the most populous places live the true wild beasts.

Choose a heroic ideal, but rather to emulate than to imitate.

BRAVE WORDS

Long as thine Art shall love true love,
Long as thy Science truth shall know,
Long as thine Eagle harms no Dove,
Long as thy Law by Law shall grow,
Long as thy God is God above,
Thy brother every man below,
So long, dear Land of all my love,
Thy name shall shine, thy fame shall glow.

SIDNEY LANIER

A Patriot's Story of Battle

by a Sergeant of the Revolutionary War

Three or four days after the victory at Trenton, the American army recrossed the Delaware into New Jersey.

At this time our troops were in a destitute and deplorable condition. The horses attached to our cannon were without shoes; and when passing over the ice they would slide in every direction; and could advance only by the assistance of the soldiers. Onr men too were without shoes or other comfortable clothing; and as traces of our march towards Princeton, the ground was literally marked with the blood of the soldiers' feet. Though my own feet did not bleed, they were so sore that their condition was little better.

While we were at Trenton, on the last of December, 1776, the time for which I and the most of my regiment had enlisted, expired. At this trying moment, General Washington, having now but a handful of men, and many of them new recruits in which he could place but little confidence, ordered our regiment to be paraded, and personally addressed us, urging that we should stay a month longer. He alluded to our recent victory at Trenton,—told us that our services were greatly needed, and that we could now do more for our country than we ever could at any future period; and in the most affectionate manner entreated us to stay. The drums beat for volunteers, but not a man turned out, The soldiers, worn down with fatigue and privations, had their hearts fixed on home and the comforts of the domestic circle, and it was hard to forego the anticipated pleasure of the society of our dearest friends.

The General wheeled his horse about,—rode through in front of the regiment, and addressing us again, said, "My brave fellows, you have done all I ever asked you to do, and more than could be reasonably expected; but your country is at stake, your wives, your houses, and all that you hold dear. You have worn yourselves out with fatigue and hardships, but we know not how to spare you. If you will consent to stay only one month longer, you will render that service to the cause of liberty and to your country, which you probably never can do under any other circumstances. The present is emphatically the *crisis* which is to decide our destiny." The drums beat the second time. The soldiers felt the force of the appeal. One said to another, I will remain if you will. Others remarked, we cannot go home under such circumstances. A few stepped forth, and their example was immediately followed by nearly all who were fit for duty in the regiment, amounting to about 200 volunteers. An officer enquired of the General if these men should be enroled. He replied,—"No: men who will volunteer in such a case as this, need no enrolment to keep them to their duty."

The Flag Goes By

by HENRY HOLCOMB BENNETT

Hats off!
Along the street there comes
A blare of bugles, a ruffle of drums,
A flash of color beneath the sky:
Hats off!
The flag is passing by!

Blue and crimson and white it shines,
Over the steel-tipped, ordered lines.
Hats off!
The colors before us fly;
But more than the flag is passing by.

Sea-fights and land-fights, grim and great,
Fought to make and to save the State:
Weary marches and sinking ships;
Cheers of victory on dying lips;

Days of plenty and years of peace;
March of a strong land's swift increase;
Equal justice, right and law,
Stately honor and reverend awe;

Sign of a nation, great and strong
To ward her people from foreign wrong:
Pride and glory and honor,—all
Live in the colors to stand or fall.

Hats off!
Along the street there comes
A blare of bugles, a ruffle of drums;
And loyal hearts are beating high:
Hats off!
The flag is passing by!

George Washington to Patrick Henry, Governor of Virginia.

Valley Forge 27th Dec. 1777

In several of my late letters I addressed you on the distress of the Troops for want of Cloathing. Your ready exertions to relieve them have given me the highest satisfaction. At the same time knowing how exceedingly the service has been injured, How great the sufferings and loss of Men thro' this want, I cannot but hope every measure will be pursued, that circumstances will admit, to keep them supplied from time to time. No pains, no efforts can be too great for this purpose. The articles of Shoes Stockings and Blankets demand the most particular attention, as the expenditure of them from the operations and common accidents of war, we find to be greater than articles of any others. I assure you Sir it is not easy to give you a just and accurate Idea of the sufferings of the Troops at large. Were they to be minutely detailed, the relation so unexpected, so contrary to the common opinion of people distant from the Army, would scarcely be thought credible. I fear I shall wound your feelings by telling you that by a Field Return on the 23d Instant, we had in Camp not less than 2898 men unfit for duty by reason of their being barefoot and otherwise naked. Besides these there are many others detained at the Hospitals and in the Farmers houses for the same causes. I will no longer dwell upon the melancholy subject, being firmly convinced that your views and most studious care will be employed to render the situation of the troops,— both officers and privates, comfortable in future. If the several States direct their attention to this indispensably essential object, as I trust they will, I have the most sanguine hopes, that their Supplies with those immediately imported by Congress themselves, will be equal to every demand.

I have the honor to be &c.

GEO. WASHINGTON.

His Excellency, PATRICK HENRY.

Second Inaugural Address
Abraham Lincoln

March 4, 1865

Probably the shortest speech of this importance in the last century

Fellow-countrymen — At this second appearing to take the oath of the Presidential office, there is less occasion for an extended address than there was at the first. Then a statement somewhat in detail of a course to be pursued seemed very fitting and proper. Now, at the expiration of four years, during which public declarations have been constantly called forth on every point and phase of the great contest which still absorbs the attention and engrosses the energies of the nation, little that is new could be presented.

The progress of our arms, upon which all else chiefly depends, is as well known to the public as to myself, and it is, I trust, reasonably satisfactory and encouraging to all. With high hope for the future, no prediction in regard to it is ventured.

On the occasion corresponding to this four years ago, all thoughts were anxiously directed to an impending civil war. All dreaded it, all sought to avoid it. While the inaugural address was being delivered from this place, devoted altogether to saving the Union without war, insurgent agents were in the city, seeking to destroy it with war — seeking to dissolve the Union and divide the effects by negotiation. Both parties deprecated war, but one of them would make war rather than let the nation survive, and the other would accept war rather than let it perish, and the war came. One-eighth of the whole population were colored slaves, not distributed generally over the Union, but localized in the southern part of it. These slaves constituted a peculiar and powerful interest. All knew that this interest was somehow the cause of the war. To strengthen, perpetuate, and extend this interest was the object for which the insurgents would rend the Union by war, while the Government claimed no right to do more than to restrict the territorial enlargement of it.

Neither party expected for the war the magnitude or the duration which it has already attained. Neither anticipated that the cause of the conflict might cease, even before the conflict itself should cease. Each looked for an easier triumph, and a result less fundamental and astounding.

Both read the same Bible and pray to the same God, and each invokes His aid against the other. It may seem strange that any men should dare to ask a just God's assistance in wringing their bread from the sweat of other men's faces, but let us judge not, that we be not judged. The prayer of both could not be answered. That of neither has been answered fully. The Almighty has His own purposes. Woe unto the world because of offences, for it must needs be that offences come, but woe to that man by whom the offence cometh. If we shall suppose that American slavery is one of these offences which, in the providence of God, must needs come, but which having continued through His appointed time, He now wills to remove, and that He gives to both North and South this terrible war as the woe due to those by whom the offence came, shall we discern there any departure from those Divine attributes which the believers in a living God always ascribe to Him? Fondly do we hope, fervently do we pray, that this mighty scourge of war may speedily pass away. Yet if God wills that it continue until all the wealth piled by the bondman's two hundred and fifty years of unrequited toil shall be sunk, and until every drop of blood drawn with the lash shall be paid by another drawn with the sword, as was said three thousand years ago, so, still it must be said, that the judgments of the Lord are true and righteous altogether.

With malice towards none, with charity for all, with firmness in the right as God gives us to see the right, let us strive on to finish the work we are in, to bind up the nation's wounds, to care for him who shall have borne the battle, and for his widow and his orphans, to do all which may achieve and cherish a just and a lasting peace among ourselves and with all nations.

* * *

Differences of race and culture are not accurate measurements of superiority or inferiority. As I see it, uniformity is something to be abhorred. The world would be a very unattractive place if everything conformed. . . . The great richness of our universe is due above all to its diversity, We should take honorable pride in the distinct accomplishments of the Irish, the French, the Asian, the Negro. We must be equally aware that the accomplishments of others are proper subjects for their pride too. These thoughts were present in each day's work. These differences were obvious and pleasing to us.

—Dr. Thomas Dooley

· 74 ·

The Monroe Doctrine

There are frequent references to this cornerstone of
American Foreign Policy but relatively few people are
aware of its origin. This developed from President
Monroe's annual message to Congress, December 2, 1823.

"It was stated at the commencement of the last session that a
great effort was then making in Spain and Portugal to improve
the condition of the people of those countries, and that it appeared to be conducted with extraordinary moderation. It need
scarcely be remarked that the result has been so far very different from what was then anticipated. Of events in that quarter of the globe, with which we have so much intercourse and
from which we derive our origin, we have always been anxious
and interested spectators. The citizens of the United States
cherish sentiments the most friendly in favor of the liberty
and happiness of their fellow-men on that side of the Atlantic.
In the wars of the European powers, in matters relating to
themselves, we have never taken any part, nor does it comport
with our policy so to do. It is only when our rights are invaded
or seriously menaced, that we resent injuries or make preparation for our defense. With the movements in this hemisphere
we are, of necessity, more immediately connected and by causes
which must be obvious to all enlightened and impartial ob-
servers. The political system of the allied powers is essentially
different in this respect from that of America. This difference
proceeds from that which exists in their respective governments. And to the defense of our own, which has been achieved
by the loss of so much blood and treasure, and matured by the
wisdom of their most enlightened citizens, and under which we
have enjoyed unexampled felicity, this whole nation is devoted.
We owe it, therefore, to candor and to the amicable relations
existing between the United States and those powers, to declare that *we should consider any attempt on their part to extend their system to any portion of this hemisphere as dangerous to our peace and safety.* With the existing colonies or
dependencies of any European power we have not interfered,
and shall not interfere. But with the governments who have
declared their independence and maintained it, and whose
independence we have, on great consideration and on just principles, acknowledged, we could not view any interposition for
the purpose of oppressing them, or controlling in any other
manner their destiny, by any European power, in any other

light than as *the manifestation of an unfriendly disposition toward the United States*. In the war between those new governments and Spain we declared our neutrality at the time of their recognition, and to this we have adhered and shall continue to adhere, provided no change shall occur which, in the judgment of the competent authorities of this government, shall make a corresponding change on the part of the United States indispensable to their security.

"The late events in Spain and Portugal show that Europe is still unsettled. Of this important fact no stronger proof can be adduced than that the allied powers should have thought it proper, on a principle satisfactory to themselves, to have interposed by force in the internal concerns of Spain. To what extent such interposition may be carried on the same principle, is a question to which all independent powers, whose governments differ from theirs, are interested; even those most remote, and surely none more so than the United States. Our policy in regard to Europe, which was adopted at an early stage of the wars which have so long agitated that quarter of the globe, nevertheless remains the same, which is, not to interfere in the internal concerns of any of its powers; to consider the government *de facto* as the legitimate government for us; to cultivate friendly relations with it, and to preserve those relations by a frank, firm, and manly policy; meeting, in all instances, the just claims of every power; submitting to injuries from none. But in regard to these continents, circumstances are eminently and conspicuously different. It is impossible that the allied powers should extend their political system to any portion of either continent without endangering our peace and happiness; nor can any one believe that our southern brethren, if left to themselves, would adopt it of their own accord. It is equally impossible, therefore, that we should behold such interposition, in any form, with indifference. If we look to the comparative strength and resources of Spain and those new governments, and their distance from each other, it must be obvious that she can never subdue them. It is still the true policy of the United States to leave the parties to themselves, in hope that other powers will pursue the same course."

The Foreign Policy of The United States

As Spelled Out by Charles Evans Hughes
More Than Fifty Years Ago

This is no time for America to yield the leadership in government which for one hundred and fifty years she has maintained, or to be ashamed, or make apology for what we are and have been. This is the time of all times when we should hold our banner high, proclaim our international ethics and assert that leadership. For this reason I shall repeat the basic principles of our foreign policy; they are brief and simple precepts which should be upon the walls of every school and college and club, and deep in the mind and heart of every child, every man and every woman. They were stated by Charles Evans Hughes, when secretary of state, to the nations of the world; he said:

"The principles of American Foreign Policy are simple and easily stated:

(1) "We do not covet any territory anywhere on God's broad earth."

What a New Testament of world policy is this, "We do not covet any territory anywhere on God's broad earth." No other nation has ever proclaimed that principle as its first principle; no other nation can declare it now. Had this been the first commandment in national diplomacy since the time of Christ, 90 per cent of all the battles that have been fought would never have been fought, and if it should be adopted by all nations now, 90 per cent of all the war problems that threaten the sky would be dissolved.

(2) "We are not seeking a sphere of economic influence and endeavoring to control others for our own aggrandizement."

And we are the only nation in the world that has made that a national policy, and no other great power can make it such without a complete reversal of their present inclinations and practices.

(3) "We are not seeking special privileges any-where at the expense of others."

Look throughout the world at the insinuating projects of other nations and their strife for privileges all their own, and you find that none other can make that declaration. These three principles negative the evils of the past; there are two positive principles upon which to construct a new international policy for the future:

(4) "We wish to protect the just and equal rights of Americans everywhere in the world."

Take that to your souls — to protect the JUST and EQUAL rights of Americans everywhere in the world; any man, or any nation that would do less is already dead in his soul.

(5) "We wish to maintain equality of commer-cial opportunity, as we call it, the 'Open Door'."

These principles are the foundation for a new world, of liberty, of equality, of fraternity and peace. Have Faith in America.

From a speech entitled *Have Faith In America* given
by Montaville Flowers at the Executives' Club
of Chicago May 25, 1928

The Story of The Stars and Stripes

by A. Y. LEECH

(By permission of "The Youth's Companion")

Relatively few Americans know the history of the Flag of the
United States.

The first national legislation pertaining to the Stars and
Stripes bears the date of June 14, 1777, when Congress, in
session at Philadelphia, adopted the following:

"*Resolved,* That the flag of the thirteen United States be
thirteen stripes, alternate red and white; that the union be
thirteen stars, white in a blue field, representing a new con-
stellation."

This was about one year subsequent to the Declaration of
Independence. Prior to that time colonial flags, and those improvised by the parties using them, were publicly displayed as
occasion demanded, but these were in no sense the "national
standard."

The thirteen stripes had been introduced in alternate white
and blue, on the upper left-hand corner of a standard presented to the Philadelphia Light Horse Company by its captain
in the early part of 1775. Moreover, the flag of the thirteen
united colonies raised at Washington's headquarters at Cam-
bridge, January 2, 1776, had the thirteen stripes just as they
are this day; but it also had the cross of St. George and St.
Andrew on a blue ground in the corner.

There is no satisfactory evidence, however, that *any* flag
bearing the union of the stars had been in public use before the
resolution of June, 1777.

Some writers assert that the first and original United States
flag, instead of thirteen stars, each representing a revolted
colony or state, contained only twelve stars, because Georgia
was not entitled to a vote. Such a flag is said to have been
made by the ladies of Philadelphia from the design of the
escutcheon of the Washington family, and it is said that Washington himself cut out the five-pointed stars.

It is alleged that this flag was presented to John Paul Jones;
that he sailed with it up and down the Schuylkill, to show the
people the appearance of the flag of their country; that it was
adopted by Congress; that Jones carried it with him on his
ship *Bonhomme Richard;* that in his great fight the flag was
shot away from its staff and fell in the sea, and that Lieutenant

Stafford leaped overboard after it, brought it safely to the ship and nailed it to the masthead.

The tale may be true, but the flag was not the national flag. The Act of Congress June 14, 1777, shows that *no* standard was recognized by the Nation until that date.

It has been impossible to decide with certainty who designed the American flag as first adopted by Congress, but the best recorded evidence gives part of the credit of designing it and all the credit of making it to Mrs. John Ross, an upholsterer, who resided on Arch Street, Philadelphia. Her descendants assert that a committee of Congress, accompanied by General Washington, who was in Philadelphia in June, 1776, called upon Mrs. Ross and engaged her to make the flag from a rough drawing. This drawing was, at her suggestion, redrawn by General Washington with pencil, in her back parlor, and the flag thus designed was adopted by Congress.

Although the resolution establishing the flag was not officially promulgated by the Secretary of Congress until September 3, 1777, it seems well authenticated that the regulation Stars and Stripes was carried at the battle of the Brandywine, September 11, 1777, and thenceforward during the battles of the Revolution.

Soon ofter its adoption the new flag was hoisted on the naval vessels of the United States. The ship *Ranger*, bearing the

Stars and Stripes, and commanded by Captain Paul Jones, arrived at a French port about December 1, 1777. Her flag received on February 14, 1778, the first salute ever paid to the American flag by foreign naval vessels.

No further action relative to the flag was taken by Congress until after Vermont and Kentucky were admitted to the Union. Then, on January 13, 1794, Congress enacted:

"That from and after the first day of May, 1795, the flag of the United States be fifteen stripes, alternate red and white; that the union be fifteen stars, white in a blue field."

This flag was the national banner from 1795 to 1818, during which period occurred the war of 1812 with Great Britain. But soon five additional states—Tennessee, Ohio, Louisiana, Indiana and Mississippi—were admitted to the Union and required representation on the flag. So Congress, on April 4, 1818, enacted:

First. "That from and after the fourth day of July next, the flag of the United States be thirteen horizontal stripes, alternate red and white; that the Union have twenty stars, white in a blue field."

Second. "That on the admission of every new state into the union one star be added to the union of the flag, and that such addition shall take effect on the Fourth of July next succeeding such admission."

The debate in Congress shows that the return to the thirteen stripes of the 1777 flag was due, in a measure, to a reverence for the standard of the Revolution; but it was also due to the fact that a further increase of the number of stripes would make the width of the flag out of porportion to its length, unless the stripes were narrowed, and this would have made it hard to see them at a distance.

A newspaper of the time, still kept in government archives, said: "By this regulation the thirteen stripes will represent the number of states whose valor and resources originally effected American independence, and additional stars will mark the increase of the states since the present Constitution."

No act has since been passed by Congress, altering this feature of the flag, and the standard is the same as originally adopted, except as to the number of stars in its union.

Letter of General Washington to Congress Urging More Pay for Nurses

From: *Medical Men in The American Revolution*
1775–1783

THE ARMY MEDICAL BULLETIN NUMBER 25
Published at the Medical Field Service School
Carlisle Barracks, Pennsylvania

Before I conclude I would beg leave to mention to Congress, that the pay now allowed to nurses for their attendance on the sick is by no means adequate to their service—the consequence of which is that they are extremely difficult to procure; indeed they are not to be got, and we are under the necessity of substituting in their place a number of men from the respective regiments, whose services by that means is entirely lost to the proper line of their duty, and but little benefit indeed to the sick. The officers I have talked with upon the subject all agree that they should be allowed a dollar a week, and that for less they cannot be had. Our sick are extremely numerous, and we find their removal attended with greatest difficulty. It is a matter that employs much of our time and care, and what makes it more distressing, is the want of proper and convenient places for their reception. I fear their sufferings will be great and many; however nothing on my part that humanity or policy can require shall be wanting to make them comfortable, so far as the state of things will permit it.

I have the honor to be &c.

GEO. WASHINGTON

A Verbatim Copy of a Battle Report from the War of 1812

[As a memorandum of the first gallant exploit of our little navy during the present war, we insert Captain Hull's official account of the capture of the British frigate Guerriere, believing that every American will read it again and again, with pride and pleasure.]

United States frigate Constitution,
off Boston Light, Aug. 30, 1812.

SIR—I have the honor to inform you that on the 19th inst. at 2 P.M. being in latitude 41, 42, and longitude 55, 48, with the Constitution under my command, a sail was discovered from the mast-head bearing E. by S. or E. S. E. but at such a distance we could not tell what she was. All sail was instantly made in chase, and soon found we came up with her. At 3 P.M. could plainly see that she was a ship on the starboard tack under easy sail, close on a wind; at half past 3 P.M. made her out to be a frigate; continued the chase until we were within about three miles, when I ordered the light sails taken in, the coursers hauled up, and the ship cleared for action. At this time the chase had backed his main topsail waiting for us to come down. As soon as the Constitution was ready for action, I bore down with an intention to bring him to close action immediately; but on our coming within gun shot she gave us a broadside and filled away and wore, giving us a broadside on the other tack, but without effect; her shot falling short. She continued wearing and manœuvering for about 3 quarters of an hour, to get a raking position, but finding she could not, she bore up, and run under her top-sails, and jib with the wind on the quarter. I immediately made sail to bring the ship up with her, and 5 minutes before 6 P.M. being alongside within half pistol shot, we commenced a heavy fire from all our guns, double shotted with round and grape and so well directed were they, and so warmly kept up, that in 15 minutes his mizen-mast went by the board and his main-yard in the slings, and the hull, rigging and sails very much torn to pieces. The fire was kept up with equal warmth for fifteen minutes longer, when his mainmast and foremast went, taking with them every spar, excepting the bowsprit; on seeing this we ceased firing, so that in thirty minutes after we got fairly along side the enemy, she surrendered, and had not a spar standing, and her hull below and above water so shattered, that a few more broadsides must have carried her down.

After informing you that so fine a ship as the Guerriere, commanded by an able and experienced officer, has been totally dismasted, and otherwise cut to pieces so as to make her not worth towing into port, in the short space of thirty minutes, you can have no doubt of the gallantry, and good conduct of the officers and ship's company I have the honor to command; it only remains therefore for me to assure you, that they all fought with great bravery; and it gives me great pleasure to say that from the smallest boy in the ship to the oldest seaman, not a look of fear was seen. They all went into action giving three cheers, and requesting to be laid close along side the enemy.

Enclosed I have the honour to send you a list of killed and wounded on board the Constitution, and a report of the damages she has sustained, also a list of killed and wounded on board the enemy, with his quarter bill &c.

I have the honour to be,
With very great respect,
Sir, your obedient servant.
ISAAC HULL.

The Hon. Paul Hamilton, &c.

[Here follows the names of those killed and wounded on board the respective ships. On board the Constitution, 7 were killed, and 7 wounded.—On board the Guerriere, 15 killed, 63 wounded and 24 *missing*. These were probably on the yards or in the tops when the masts were shot away.—Total killed, wounded and missing on board the Guerriere, 102.]

John Adams Expressing His Views of the Future Needs of the United States

From his inaugural address

I venture to say, that if a preference, upon principle, of a free republican government, formed upon long and serious reflection, after a diligent and impartial inquiry after truth; if an attachment to the Constitution of the United States, and a conscientious determination to support it, until it shall be altered by the judgments and wishes of the people, expressed in the mode prescribed in it; if a respectful attention to the constitutions of the individual states, and a constant caution and delicacy toward the state governments; if an equal and impartial regard to the rights, interests, honor, and happiness of all the states of the Union, without preference or regard to a northern or southern, eastern or western position, their various political opinions on essential points, or their personal attachments; if a love of virtuous men, of all parties and denominations; if a love of science and letters, and a wish to patronize every rational effort to encourage schools, colleges, universities, academies, and every institution for propagating knowledge, virtue, and religion among all classes of the people, not only for their benign influence on the happiness of life, in all its stages and classes, and of society in all its forms, but as the only means of preserving our Constitution from its natural enemies, the spirit of sophistry, the spirit of party, the spirit of intrigue, profligacy, and corruption, and the pestilence of foreign influence, which is the angel of destruction to elective governments; if a love of equal laws, of justice and humanity, in the interior administration; if an inclination to improve agriculture, commerce, and manufactures for necessity, convenience, and defense; if a spirit of equity and humanity toward the aboriginal nations of America, and a disposition to ameliorate their condition, by inclining them to be more friendly to us, and our citizens to be more friendly to them; if an inflexible determination to maintain peace and inviolable faith with all nations, and that system of neutrality and impartiality among the belligerent powers of Europe which has been adopted by the government, and so solemnly sanctioned by both houses of Congress, and applauded by the legislatures of the states and the public opinion, until it shall be otherwise ordained by Congress; if a personal esteem for the French nation, formed in a residence of seven years chiefly among them, and a sincere desire to preserve the friendship which has been so much for the honor and interest of both nations; if, while the conscious honor and integrity of the people of America, and the internal sentiment of their own power and energies must be preserved, and earnest endeavor to investigate every just cause, and remove every colorable pretense of complaint; if an intention to pursue, by amicable negotiation, a reparation for the injuries that have been committed on the commerce of our fellow citizens, by whatever nation; and if success cannot be obtained, to lay the facts before the legislature, that they may consider what further measures the honor and interest of the government and its constituents demand... can enable me, in any degree, to comply with your wishes, it shall be my strenuous endeavor that this sagacious injunction of the two houses shall not be without effect.

★ ★ ★ ★ ★ ★ ★

A man after he has travelled over this country and seen his fellow citizens in distant parts of the continent is ashamed of himself for having been so narrow a creature before he travelled, for having thought such ignorant thoughts and such superior thoughts about his fellow citizens. The best dose for the man who would be a thinking man is to see the people he is thinking about.

— WOODROW WILSON

A new age is before us, in which, it would seem, we must lead the world.

From the inaugural address as president of Princeton University, October 25, 1902.

— WOODROW WILSON

The chief glory of a university is the leadership of the nation in the things that attach to the highest ambitions that nations can set themselves, those ideals which lift nations into the atmosphere of things that are permanent and do not fade from generation to generation. I do not see how any man can fail to perceive that scholarship, that education, in a country like ours, is a branch of statesmanship.

— WOODROW WILSON

"There is no such good luck in store for me as the Presidency"—A. Lincoln

In December 1858 Jesse W. Fell, a political associate from Bloomington, Illinois, asked Lincoln for an account of his life, to be used by Joseph J. Lewis of West Chester, Pennsylvania, "to get up a newspaper article to tell people who you are and what you have done." Fell believed there would be an excellent chance of Lincoln's becoming the Republican candidate for President in 1860 if he were better known. Lincoln refused the request and reportedly said, "Fell, I admit that I am ambitious and would like to be President, but there is no such good luck in store for me as the Presidency . . . besides, there is nothing in my early history that would interest you or anybody else." Lincoln later changed his mind, and on December 9, 1859 sent the requested sketch.

* * * * * * * *

I was born February 12, 1809, in Hardin County, Kentucky. My parents were both born in Virginia of undistinguished families, second families, perhaps I should say. My mother, who died in my tenth year, was of a family of the name of Hanks, some of whom now reside in Salem, and some others in Macon County, Illinois.

My paternal grandfather, Abraham Lincoln, emigrated from Rockingham County,Virginia, to Kentucky about 1781 or 1782, where a year or two later he was killed by Indians, not in battle, but by stealth, when he was laboring to open a farm in the forest. His ancestors, who were Quakers, went to Virginia from Bucks County, Pennsylvania. An effort to identify them with the New England family of the same name ended in nothing more definite than a similarity of Christian names in both families, such as Enoch, Levi, Mordecai, Solomon, Abraham, and the like.

My father, at the death of his father, was but six years old, and he grew up literally without education. He removed from Kentucky to what is now Spencer County, Indiana, and in my eighth year, we reached our new home about the time the state came into the Union. It was a wild region with many bears and other wild animals still in the woods. There I grew up.

There were some schools, so-called, but no qualifications were ever required of a teacher beyond reading, writing and ciphers to the Rule of Threes. If a straggler supposed to understand Latin happened to sojourn in the neighborhood he was looked upon as a wizard. There was absolutely nothing to excite ambition for education. Of course when I came of age I did not know much. Still, somehow, I could read, write, and cipher to the Rule of Three, but that was all! I have not been to school since. The little advance I now have upon this store of education I have picked up from time to time under pressure of necessity.

I was raised to farm work, which I continued till I was twenty-two. At twenty-one I came to Illinois and passed the first year in Macon County. Then I got to New Salem, at that time in Sangamon, now in Menard County, where I remained a year as a sort of clerk in a store. Then came the Blackhawk War and I was elected Captain of Volunteers, a success which gave me more pleasure than any I have had since. I went through the campaign and later ran for the legislature, in the year 1832, and was beaten—the only time I have been beaten by the people. The next, and three succeeding biennial elections, I was elected to the legislature. I was not a candidate afterward.

During this legislative period I had studied law, and removed to Springfield to practice it. In 1841 I was elected to the House of Congress, was not a candidate for reelection. From 1849 to 1854, both inclusive, I practiced law more assiduously than ever before. Always a Whig in politics and generally on the Whig electoral ticket making active canvasses, I was losing interest in politics, when the repeal of the Missouri Compromise aroused me again. What I have done since then is pretty well known.

If any description of me is thought desirable, it may be said, I am in height six feet four inches nearly, lean in flesh, weighing an average, one hundred eighty pounds, dark complexion with coarse black hair, and grey eyes. No other marks or brands recollected.

Springfield Dec. 20, 1859

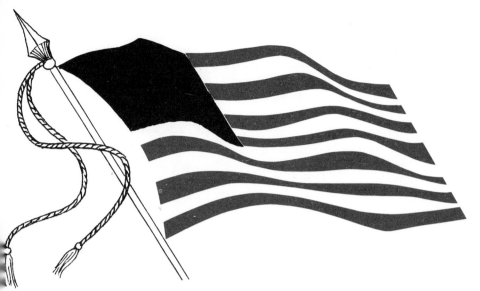

"Our Flag Was Still There"

"You will remember that in 1814, when *The Star-Spangled Banner* was written, I resided in Frederic, and Mr. Key in Georgetown. Soon after the British troops retired from Washington, a squadron of the enemy's ships made their way up the Potomac and appeared before Alexandria, which was compelled to capitulate. The squadron remained there some days, plundering the town of tobacco, and whatever else they wanted. It was rumored, and believed in Frederic, that a marauding attack of the same character would be made on Georgetown and Washington, before the ships left the river. Mr. Key's family was still in Georgetown. He would not, and indeed could not, with honor, leave the place while it was threatened by the enemy for he was a volunteer in the light artillery."

In these words, the brother-in-law of Francis Scott Key begins the story of the events that led to the writing of *The Star-Spangled Banner*. He explained that because of Key's affiliation with the Army, as a volunteer, he was sought out by friends of a well known physician, a Dr. Beanes, who had been seized as a prisoner by the British, as they withdrew from the Washington area headed for Baltimore. Key agreed to undertake the mission of boarding the British ships under a flag of truce to obtain the release of Dr. Beanes.

He found the British fleet at the mouth of the Potomac preparing for the expedition against Baltimore. He was courteously received by Admirals Cochrane and Cockburn of the

British fleet. They agreed to release the doctor because of reports of his kind treatment of wounded British soldiers and sailors whom they had been compelled to leave behind when they withdrew from Washington. However, neither Key nor Dr. Beanes would be released until after the assault on the city of Baltimore and Fort McHenry. Thus, on the day and night of the attack Key and the doctor had a view of the action at close range from the deck of a British vessel.

They were anchored in a position which enabled them to see the flag of Fort McHenry. Key remained on deck during the early evening watching the shells and listening to the explosions. Suddenly the bombardment ceased and he and Dr. Beanes had no way of knowing whether or not the fort had surrendered. They paced the deck the rest of the night. Just at dawn, before they could clearly see objects at a distance, they strained their eyes in the direction of the fort. Through the haze they could still make out the Stars and Stripes, a thrilling sight which told them that the fort had not surrendered.

"Our flag was still there." As the day advanced they discovered, from the movements of the boats between the shore and the fleet, that the British troops had suffered many casualties, judging from the wounded who were being brought aboard the ships.

Inspired by the action of the night and early morning, Key had written *The Star-Spangled Banner*. He said he began to write in the evening during the fervor of the moment when he saw the enemy hastily retreating to their ships and looked at the flag he had watched for so anxiously, as the dawn approached. He wrote some lines and made some notes upon the back of a letter which he happened to have in his pocket. Some of the lines he kept in his mind, to be written down while he was in the boat that took him to shore. Key wrote it out completely at the hotel in Baltimore where he spent the next night. For the music, he adapted the words to a popular English tune of that period entitled *To Anacreon in Heaven*.

The next morning he took it to a friend, Judge Nicholson of the Maryland Court of Appeals. The Judge was so favorably impressed that he immediately took it to a printer and ordered copies to be produced in the form of handbills. Thus the great national anthem was first published.

Although he was not a noted poet, Francis Scott Key did have poems other than *The Star-Spangled Banner* published.

The Pony Express

From *Roughing It* — by Mark Twain

In a little while all interest was taken up in stretching our necks and watching for the "pony-rider"—the fleet messenger who sped across the continent from St. Joe to Sacramento, carrying letters nineteen hundred miles in eight days! Think of that for perishable horse and human flesh and blood to do! The pony-rider was usually a little bit of a man, brimful of spirit and endurance. No matter what time of the day or night his watch came on, and no matter whether it was winter or summer, raining, snowing, hailing, or sleeting, or whether his "beat" was a level straight road or a crazy trail over mountain crags and precipices, or whether it led through peaceful regions or regions that swarmed with hostile Indians, he must be always ready to leap into the saddle and be off like the wind! There was no idling-time for a pony-rider on duty. He rode fifty miles without stopping, by daylight, moonlight, starlight, or through the blackness of darkness—just as it happened. He rode a splendid horse that was born for a racer and fed and lodged like a gentleman; kept him at his utmost speed for ten miles, and then, as he came crashing up to the station where stood two men holding fast a fresh, impatient steed, the transfer of rider and mail-bag was made in the twinkling of an eye, and away flew the eager pair and were out of sight before the spectator could get hardly the ghost of a look. Both rider and horse went "flying light." The rider's dress was thin, and fitted close; he wore a "roundabout," and a skull-cap, and tucked his pantaloons into his boot-tops like a race-rider. He carried no arms—he carried nothing that was not absolutely necessary, for even the postage on his literary freight was worth *five dol-*

lars a letter. He got but little frivolous correspondence to carry —his bag had business letters in it mostly. His horse was stripped of all unnecessary weight, too. He wore light shoes, or none at all. The little flat mail-pockets strapped under the rider's thighs would each hold about the bulk of a child's primer. They held many and many an important business chapter and newspaper letter, but these were written on paper as airy and thin as goldleaf, nearly, and thus bulk and weight were economized. The stage-coach traveled about a hundred to a hundred and twenty-five miles a day (twenty-four hours), the pony-rider about two hundred and fifty. There were about eighty pony-riders in the saddle all the time, night and day, stretching in a long, scattering procession from Missouri to California, forty flying eastward, and forty toward the west, and among them making four hundred gallant horses earn a stirring livelihood and see a deal of scenery every single day in the year.

We had had a consuming desire, from the beginning, to see a pony-rider, but somehow or other all that passed us and all that met us managed to streak by in the night, and so we heard only a whiz and a hail, and the swift phantom of the desert was gone before we could get our heads out of the windows. But now we were expecting one along every moment, and would see him in broad daylight. Presently the driver exclaims:

"HERE HE COMES!"

Every neck is stretched further, and every eye strained wider. Away across the endless dead level of the prairie a black speck appears against the sky, and it is plain that it moves. Well, I should think so! In a second or two it becomes a horse and rider, rising and falling, rising and falling—sweeping toward us nearer and nearer—growing more and more distinct, more and more sharply defined—nearer and still nearer, and the flutter of the hoofs comes faintly to the ear—another instant a whoop and a hurrah from our upper deck, a wave of the rider's hand, but no reply, and man and horse burst past our excited faces, and go swinging away like a belated fragment of a storm!

So sudden is it all, and so like a flash of unreal fancy, that but for the flake of white foam left quivering and perishing on a mail-sack after the vision had flashed by and disappeared, we might have doubted whether we had seen any actual horse and man at all, maybe.

Life Can Signify Much

by DR. THOMAS DOOLEY

In college we were taught the ubiquity of God. But to see God in all things when you are plunged into bleating materialism is sometimes hard. I certainly cannot see God when I look at a Mercedes Benz convertible. But in the jungle it is easier. Here we can know God a little better. Perhaps it is because of solitude. We can see God in the tropic rain, in the monsoon mud, in the tangy sweet smell of the earth that comes upon us as we walk amongst the mountains. The mimosa, the frangipani, the tamarind trees, the thatched roof, the quiet peace of the hills and valleys, the cool refreshment of the river, the surge of the night, the bustling of the market place. God is more intimately present in us than we realize. We ought to shut up a few minutes and seek Him. Life can signify much. We must just listen to the voices which are inside each of us. All we need to do is listen more acutely, rub our eyes and see things a bit better. If the light is seen, if the sweet odor is grasped, if the sound is heard, then a man's whole being is caught up in soul-satisfying contentment.

A man working in this world without tapping his own reservoir of spiritual strength is like a twin-engined plane flying with only one motor. He may get there, but it will be mighty difficult. Often, late at night, Bob, John, and I would kneel beside our cots and pray the family rosary out loud. Our whole job took on a new meaning when we remembered the words, "Inasmuch as ye have done it unto the least of these, my brethren, ye have done it unto Me."

> *Give us, Thy worthy children,*
> *The blessings of wisdom and speech,*
> *And the hands and hearts of healing*
> *And the lips and tongues that teach.*

(The prayer which served as inspiration to Dr. Tom Dooley and his co-workers in Laos.)

General Lee and His Faithful *Traveller*

From: *Recollections and Letters of General Robert E. Lee*
by His Son, CAPTAIN ROBERT E. LEE

How is Traveller? Tell him I miss him dreadfully, and have repented of our separation but once—and that is the whole time since we parted."

I think Traveller appreciated his love and sympathy, and returned it as much as was in a horse's nature to do. As illustrative of this bond between them, a very pretty story was told me by Mrs. S. P. Lee*:

"One afternoon in July of this year, the General rode down to the canal-boat landing to put on board a young lady who had been visiting his daughters and was returning home. He dismounted, tied Traveller to a post, and was standing on the boat making his adieux, when someone called out that Traveller was loose. Sure enough, the gallant gray was making his way up the road, increasing his speed as a number of boys and men tried to stop him. My father immediately stepped ashore, called to the crowd to stand still, and advancing a few steps gave a peculiar low whistle. At the first sound, Traveller stopped and pricked up his ears. The General whistled a second time, and the horse with a glad whinny turned and trotted quietly back to his master, who patted and coaxed him before tying him up again. To a bystander expressing surprise at the creature's docility the General observed that he did not see how any man could ride a horse for any length of time without a perfect understanding being established between them. My sister Mildred, who rode with him constantly this summer, tells me of his enjoyment of their long rides out into the beautiful, restful country. Nothing seemed to delight him so much.

"I have often known him to give rein to Traveller and go at gull speed to the top of some long hill, then turn and wait for me jogging along on Lucy, calling out with merry voice, 'Come along, Miss Lucy, Lucy Long!' He would question the country people about the roads, where they came from, where they led to, and soon knew every farmer's name and every homestead in the country. He often said:

" 'I wish I had a little farm of my own, where we could live in peace to the end of our days. You girls could attend to the

---

*Daughter of General W. N. Pendleton, Chief of Artillery of the A. N. Va., and widow of Colonel Edwin Grey Lee, C. S.A.

dairy and the cows and the sheep and wait on your mother and me, for it is time now for us old people to rest and for the young people to work.' "

All the children in the country around were devoted to him, and felt no hesitation in approaching him, after they once knew him. He used to meet his favorites among the little ones on the street, and would sometimes lift them up in front of him to give them a ride on Traveller. That was the greatest treat he could provide. There is a very pretty story told of Virginia Lee Letcher, his god daughter, and her baby sister, Fannie, which is yet remembered among the Lexington people. Jennie had been followed by her persistent sister, and all the coaxing and the commanding of the six-year-old failed to make the younger return home. Fannie had sat down by the roadside to pout, When General Lee came riding by. Jennie at once appealed to him:

"General Lee, won't you please make this child go home to her mother?"

The General immediately rode over to where Fannie sat, leaned over from his saddle and drew her up into his lap. There she sat in royal contentment, and was thus grandly escorted home. When Mrs. Letcher inquired of Jennie why she had given General Lee so much trouble, she received the naive reply:

"I couldn't make Fan go home, and I thought *he* could do anything."*

———

*Daughter of Governor John Letcher—the War Governor of Virginia.

ALEXANDER HAMILTON EXPLAINS THE
FOUNDATION OF THE POWER OF THE
UNITED STATES SUPREME COURT

From *The Federalist*

There is no position which depends on clearer principles, than that every act of a delegated authority, contrary to the tenor of the commission under which it is exercised, is void. No legislative act, therefore, contrary to the Constitution, can be valid. To deny this, would be to affirm, that the deputy is greater than his principal; that the servant is above his master; that the representatives of the people are superior to the people themselves; that men acting by virtue of powers, may do not only what their powers do not authorize, but what they forbid.

If it be said that the legislative body are themselves the constitutional judges of their own powers, and that the construction they put upon them is conclusive upon the other departments, it may be answered, that this cannot be the natural presumption, where it is not to be collected from any particular provisions in the Constitution. It is not otherwise to be supposed, that the Constitution could intend to enable the representatives of the people to substitute their *will* to that of their constituents. It is far more rational to suppose, that the courts were designed to be an intermediate body between the people and the legislature, in order, among other things, to keep the latter within the limits assigned to their authority. The interpretation of the laws is the proper and peculiar province of the courts. A constitution is, in fact, and must be regarded by the judges, as a fundamental law. It therefore belongs to them to ascertain its meaning, as well as the meaning of any particular act proceeding from the legislative body. If there should happen to be an irreconcilable variance between the two, that which has the superior obligation and validity ought, of course, to be preferred; or, in other words, the Constitution ought to be preferred to the statute, the intention of the people to the intention of their agents.

Nor does this conclusion by any means suppose a superiority of the judicial to the legislative power. It only supposes that the power of the people is superior to both; and that where the will of the legislature, declared in its statutes, stands in opposition to that of the people, declared in the Constitution, the judges ought to be governed by the latter rather than the former. They ought to regulate their decisions by the fundamental laws, rather than by those which are not fundamental...

If, then, the courts of justice are to be considered as the bulwarks of a limited Constitution against legislative encroachments, this consideration will afford a strong argument for the permanent tenure of judicial offices, since nothing will contribute so much as this to that independent spirit in the judges which must be essential to the faithful performance of so arduous a duty.

* * *

JAMES OTIS—GUIDING SPIRIT OF FREEDOM
—— 1761 ——
From the letters of JOHN ADAMS to William Tudor

Otis was a flame of fire!—with a promptitude of classical allusions, a depth of research, a rapid summary of historical events and dates, a profusion of legal authorities, a prophetic glance of his eye into futurity, and a torrent of impetuous eloquence, he hurried away every thing before him. American independence was then and there born; the seeds of patriots and heroes were then and there sown, to defend the vigorous youth, the *non sine Diis animosus infans.* Every man of a crowded audience appeared to me to go away, as I did, ready to take arms against Writs of Assistance. Then and there was the first scene of the first act of opposition to the arbitrary claims of Great Britain. Then and there the child Independence was born. In fifteen years, namely in 1776, he grew up to manhood, and declared himself free. . . .

James Otis was descended from our most ancient families. His education was the best his country afforded. He was bred to the bar under Mr. Gridley, the greatest lawyer and the greatest classic scholar I ever knew at any bar. His application was incessant and indefatigable. Justice Richard Dana has often told me, that the apartment in which Otis studied, when a pupil and a clerk of Mr. Gridley, was near his house; that he had watched him from day to day, and that he had never known a student in law so punctual, so steady, so constant and persevering. Accordingly, as soon as he was admitted to the bar, he became a conspicuous figure. And among whom? Gridley, Pratt, Trowbridge; and he was much admired, and as much celebrated as any of them. His generous, manly, noble character, as a private gentleman, his uncommon attainments in literature, especially in the law, and his nervous, commanding eloquence at the bar, were everywhere spoken of.

"JUDGES ARE BUT MEN"

An extract from an address delivered in the United States Senate
by CHARLES SUMNER, Republican Senator from Massachusetts

Let me here say that I hold Judges, and especially the Supreme
Court of the country, in much respect; but I am too familiar
with the history of judicial proceedings to regard them with any
superstitious reverence. Judges are but men, and in all ages
have shown a full share of frailty. Alas! alas! the worst crimes
of history have been perpetrated under their sanction. The
blood of martyrs and of patriots, crying from the ground, sum-
mons them to judgment.

It was a judicial tribunal which condemned Socrates to drink
the fatal hemlock, and which pushed the Saviour barefoot over
the pavements of Jerusalem, bending beneath his cross. It was
a judicial tribunal which, against the testimony and entreaties
of her father, surrendered the fair Virginia as a slave; which arrested the teachings of the apostle to the Gentiles, and sent
him in bonds from Judea to Rome; which in the name of old
religion, adjudged the saints and fathers of the Christian
Church to death, in all its most dreadful forms; and which
afterwards in the name of the new religion, enforced the tor-
tures of the Inquisition, amidst the shrieks and agonies of its
victims; while it compelled Galileo to declare, in solemn denial
of the great truth he had disclosed, that the earth did not
move round the sun.

. . . Ay, sir, it was a judicial tribunal in England, surrounded
by all the forms of law, which sanctioned every despotic caprice
of Henry the Eighth, from the unjust divorce of his queen to
the beheading of Sir Thomas More; which lighted the fires of
persecution, that glowed at Oxford and Smithfield, over the
cinders of Latimer, Ridley, and John Rodgers; which, after
elaborate argument, upheld the fatal tyranny of ship money
against the patriotic resistance of Hampden . . . which persistently enforced the laws of conformity that our Puritan
fathers persistently refused to obey; and which afterwards,
with Jeffries on the bench, crimsoned the pages of English
history with massacre and murder, even with the blood of innocent women. Ay, sir, and it was a judicial tribunal in our
country, surrounded by all the forms of law, which hung witches
at Salem, which affirmed the constitutionality of the Stamp Act,
while it admonished "jurors and the people" to obey; and which
now, in our day, has lent its sanction to the unutterable atrocity
of the Fugitive Slave Law.

AMERICAN FOREIGN POLICY AT WORK

from an address *by* PRESIDENT DWIGHT D. EISENHOWER · May 21, 1957

We have, during this century, twice spent our blood and our treasure fighting in Europe — and twice in Asia. We fought because we saw—too late to prevent war—that our own peace and security were imperilled, by the urgent danger — or the ruthless conquest — of other lands.

We have gained wisdom from that suffering. We know, and the world knows, that the American people will fight hostile and aggressive despotisms when their force is thrown against the barriers of freedom, when they seek to gain the high ground of power for which to destroy us. But we also know that to fight is the most costly way to keep America secure and free. Even an America victorious in atomic war could scarcely escape disastrous destruction of her cities and a fearful loss of life. Victory itself could be agony.

Plainly, we must seek less tragic, less costly ways to defend ourselves. We must recognize that whenever any country falls under the domination of Communism, the strength of the Free World — and of America — is by that amount weakened and Communism strengthened. If this process, through our neglect or indifference, should proceed unchecked, our continent would be gradually encircled. Our safety depends upon recognition of the fact that the Communist design for such encirclement must be stopped before it gains momentum — before it is again too late to save the peace.

This recognition dictates two tasks. We must maintain a common world-wide defense against the menace of International Communism. And we must demonstrate and spread the blessings of liberty — to be cherished by those who enjoy these blessings, to be sought by those now denied them.

This is not a new policy nor a partisan policy.

This is a policy for America that began ten years ago when a Democratic President and a Republican Congress united in an historic declaration. They then declared that the independence and survival of two countries menaced by Communist aggression — Greece and Turkey — were so important to the security of America that we would give them military and economic aid.

That policy saved those nations. And it did so without the cost of American lives.

That policy has since been extended to all critical areas of the world. It recognizes that America cannot exist as an island of freedom in a surrounding sea of Communism. It is expressed concretely by mutual security treaties embracing 42 other nations. And these treaties reflect a solemn finding by the President and by the Senate that our own peace would be endangered if any of these countries were conquered by International Communism.

★   ★   ★

The fact is that our foreign policy is now and will be for generations the paramount, the absorbing question before us, and upon its wise solution will depend the domestic welfare of the American people.

—WENDELL L. WILLKIE

We must never forget that international friendship is achieved through rumors ignored, propaganda challenged and exposed, through patient loyalty to those who have proved themselves worthy of it, through help freely given, where help is needed and merited. Peace is more a product of our day-to-day living than of a spectacular program, intermittently executed.

—DWIGHT D. EISENHOWER

The American people have never before faced the necessity of persisting in a foreign policy that requires time, patience and unlimited sacrifice if it is to be successful. Yet, I see no way now of avoiding this necessity if the safety of the United States is to be assured.

—SUMNER WELLES

THE
SPIRIT
OF
SPORT

The Circus-Day Parade

by JAMES WHITCOMB RILEY

Oh the Circus-Day parade! How the bugles played and
    played!
And how the glossy horses tossed their flossy manes, and
    neighed,
As the rattle and the rhyme of the tenor-drummer's time
Filled all the hungry hearts of us with melody sublime!

How the grand band-wagon shone with a splendor all its own,
And glittered with a glory that our dreams had never known!
And how the boys behind, high and low of every kind,
Marched in unconscious capture, with a rapture undefined!

How the horsemen, two and two, with their plumes of white
    and blue,
And crimson, gold and purple, nodding by at me and you,
Waved the banners that they bore, as the Knights in days of
    yore,
Till our glad eyes gleamed and glistened like the spangles that
    they wore!

How the graceless-graceful strides of the elephant was eyed,
And the capers of the little horse that cantered at his side!
How the shambling camels, tame to the plaudits of their fame,
With listless eyes came silent, masticating as they came.

How the cages jolted past, with each wagon battened fast,
And the mystery within it only hinted of at last
From the little grated square in the rear, and nosing there
The snout of some strange animal that sniffed the outer air!

And, last of all, The Clown, making mirth for all the town,
With his lips curved ever upward and his eyebrows ever down,
And his chief attention paid to the little mule that played
A tattoo on the dashboard with his heels, in the parade.

Oh! the Circus-Day parade! How the bugles played and played!
And how the glossy horses tossed their flossy manes and
    neighed,
As the rattle and the rhyme of the tenor-drummer's time
Filled all the hungry hearts of us with melody sublime!

The Origin of Professional Baseball

by A. G. Spalding

The name Spalding has for an entire century been synonymous with sport. In the 1860's and 1870's he was a leading under-hand pitcher. In those days the rules forbade overhand pitching. In the years 1872 through 1875 he starred for Boston, and in 1876 his pitching helped win the pennant for the Chicago White Stockings.

After his active career had ended, his business firm of A. G. Spalding and Company was one of the leading sporting goods companies in the world. Because of this interesting background as an early participant and star in what has become one of the great national sports of the United States, the story of the early history of baseball, as told by Spalding, is interesting to most sport fans.

In the Spalding Guide of 1905 he wrote about his early association with baseball as follows:

"I am indebted for my first acquaintance with baseball to a disabled Illinois soldier returning from the war in 1863, when as a lad of 13, I listened to his account of baseball as played in the camp and under this old soldier's coaching, I became a member of the boys' club in Rockford, Illinois, which I believe was one of the first baseball clubs organized in the West.

"From 1865 to 1870 baseball clubs sprang up everywhere and the rivalry between cities became intense. The National Club of Washington was the first Eastern club to make an extended trip through the West in 1867 and met with only one defeat, and that at the hands of the Rockford Club, at which I had the honor to be the pitcher. The result of this game was the indirect cause of my afterward becoming a professional player.

"Every effort was made at this period to keep the game on an amateur basis, but the rivalries between cities became so intense and the demand of the high-class public so urgent, that it was utterly impossible to keep the game on a strictly amateur plane. Veiled professionalism became the order of the day, and while the amateur status was insisted upon in the rules, young men possessed of skill as ball players, were offered lucrative positions in commercial houses with the understanding that they could play baseball all they wanted to, yet a large part of their salaries were provided by the local club or by some of its enthusiastic members.

"I recall my own experience when in the fall of 1867 I was surprised with an offer of a salary of $40 a week as a bill clerk in a wholesale grocery house in Chicago, which I accepted with the innocent satisfaction that my business abilities were so highly appreciated. I learned afterwards that the business concern appraised my service at $10 per week and that the Baseball Club made up the balance. This so-called amateurism or veiled professionalism, was in general vogue throughout the country during the latter part of the decade of the sixties, and it became so intolerable to players and club officials that it finally resulted in the organization of the National Association of Professional Baseball Players in 1876. From this date baseball playing has been recognized as a regular profession, and the game has since been under the management and control of regularly organized professional clubs, banded together in associations and leagues."

WHAT IS THE GREATEST SINGLE THING
IN MAKING A GREAT PLAYER?

From a speech entitled *The Greatest Single Thing a Man Can Have*
given by Branch Rickey at the Executives' Club of Chicago
November 12, 1926

What is the greatest single thing in making a great player? I think it was the same year that we were playing the Detroit Tigers at Detroit. We lost the game that day by a score of three to two. I remember in the 11th inning, when the Detroit players came to bat, I called Carl, the pitcher, over to me and asked: "Do you know the third hitter in this inning?"

"Yes, I do," he said.

"You will get the first two fellows, but don't pass that third fellow."

He was a great base runner and champion base stealer. His name was Cobb—C-o-b-b. You have heard of him, and I have wished many a day that I had not heard of him. I did not want them to walk him. I wanted them to make him hit.

Apparently Carl did not think much of the suggestion, because he did walk him. I can see that tantalizing way that Ty had; he looked like he was going to run down to second. Carl threw the ball over. He had taken his position, he had a movement and a stance that was very indecisive. You could not tell what he was going to do. Carl threw the ball over and he made a slide to the bag and the umpire paid no attention. Sometimes they are right; he was on this occasion.

Then Leary caught the comedy and threw the ball high. When Cobb ran way out, Weilman saw his chance and threw the ball, and Cobb slid in. The umpire said he was safe, although it was a closer play than the other. Leary then pretended to throw the ball higher and finally Cobb ran way out, and a second time back again.

I thought it better to get Cobb going backward than forward, so suggested that he throw the ball higher. I ought never to have said it. I make a mistake; Leary made a mistake. He never should have obeyed his manager on that occasion. He threw the ball higher just as Cobb ran way out the third time —but he never came back. He kept right on running. The man on first just reached the ball on the end of his finger but did not catch it. He picked it up quickly and hesitated.

There was no one to take it at second base. There was a little fellow there who was a graduate of the medical department of the University of Michigan, John Levan. He was the shortstop. Can't you hear him saying to himself: "Oh, come on, Weil, you can't catch Cobb. Come on, Leary, you can't catch Cobb. Let us get the hitters."

Well, when the ball was finally thrown to second base, it hit in front of the bag and bounced over Levan's head. Cobb came down, touched second base, and angularly went on towards third without a ghost of a chance to make it. The third baseman, knowing the abandonment of that fellow Cobb, and his slide—knowing that, when he set out voluntarily to get an objective, he was willing to pay the price to get it—having this knowledge in his head, had one eye on Cobb's shiny spikes and the other eye on the ball.

I then saw the quickest reflex action I ever saw in my life. That boy Cobb had reflex centers in his heels; he did not have time to telegraph his brain. He slid 12 feet in front of third base; and when the dust had cleared away, the ball had fallen out of the hands of the third baseman and was going over toward the concrete in front of the grandstand—and before we could get that ball, he scored. I saw the crowd tumbling out from every place.

I said to the umpire: "Interference, interference, Tom, at third base. He did not make a slide for the base, but he made a play for the ball."

He paid no attention to me—they have a habit of doing that. I followed him and said: "Tom, listen to me!"

"Mr. Rickey," he said then, "listen to me. Give the boy credit. He made his own breaks."

Oh, I tell you as I went down towards the clubhouse, with the crowd joshing me and guying us, I thought to myself, as I passed the Detroit players, I did not hear a man saying, "See what luck did for us today. Old Billiken was on our side." I heard everybody saying, "He is a great player. He won the game by himself."

As I came to my locker and listened to the remarks about the game, I commenced to ask myself what it was that made a man a distinguished ballplayer. Take two men with equal ability; one of them will always stay in mediocrity and another will distinguish himself in the game. What is the difference?

The more we compress and confine the element of luck—luck has its place in games, it is in the English language; it is in the dictionary, and we ought to keep it there—and put

it in a small area, just to that extent do you enlarge the area for the exercise of a man's own functions in controlling his workings, his destinies and his game.

The more that a man exercises himself and asserts his own influence over his work, the less the part that luck plays. It is true in baseball that the greatest single menace that a man has is a willingness to alibi his own failures; the greatest menace to a man's success in business, I think, sometimes is a perfect willingness to excuse himself for his own mistakes.

What is the greatest single thing in the character of a successful enterprise, in the character of a boy, in the character of a great baseball player? I think it is the desire to be a great baseball player, a desire that dominates him, a desire that is so strong that it does not admit of anything that runs counter to it, a desire to excel that so confines him to a single purpose that nothing else matters.

That thing makes men come in at night, that makes men have good health, that makes men change their bad technique to good technique, that makes capacity and ability in men. That makes a team with 80 per cent possibility come from 60 to 70 per cent, that makes them approach their possibility; and with a dominant desire to excel, that simply transcends them into a great spiritual force.

The greatest single thing in the qualification of a great player, a great team, or a great man, is a desire to reach the objective that admits of no interference anywhere. That is the greatest thing I know about baseball or anything else.

Knute Rockne's Philosophy on Sport

From a speech entitled *Athletics and Leadership*
given by Knute Rockne at the Executives' Club of Chicago, May 29, 1925

I do believe in leadership of the right kind. By that I mean that every one of us should be a leader. I believe that a sense of fairness in all things, respect for honesty and a basis for mutual understanding is the very fundamental of organized society. I do believe that athletics does build and create character, and character is the basis of leadership.

President Lowell of Harvard, said one time that young men may sometimes go astray, but as long as they are physically fit they can always come back, and some men say that the function of athletics is to keep young men physically fit. I believe that end is very desirable. Athletics does fill that end, but I do not believe that is the prime importance of athletics.

Another gentleman who has spent a lifetime in playground work said that the critical part of a day for a young fellow, for the young boy growing up, particularly in his years of adolescence, is at that time of day when he is taking his recreation—the hours when he is playing. He seems to take the point of view that athletics satisfies the normal desire of the undergraduate to play. I believe it probably fulfills that end, but that is not the point that I am going to make.

If two of us had an engagement to play tennis or some other game, whether or not we cheated, whether or not we kept physically fit, whether or not we had any skill, would be nobody's business but our own. However, if a group of us go out to represent, we will say, Notre-Dame or Northwestern University, then we bring into the situation the matter of representation and we take onto ourselves a responsibility. We are responsible to the school or to the institution which we are representing, whether or not we have any skill, whether or not we do something which might not keep us physically fit, and we have to bear the responsibilities to be sure that we do not do anything unsportsmanlike so as to reflect on the institution we represent. I think that competition on the athletic field, under proper control and supervision and development, does offer a field for character-development that is bound to make for good leadership.

I believe that the athleic field is the laboratory where a young man can acquire these things. In an athletic contest a young man has to have complete command and control of himself. He must have an intense desire to fill a certain end. He must be able to mobilize all his skill, intelligence, and courage quickly and decisively, and yet against strenuous opposition. He must always have in mind respect for the other fellow's rights and respect for the rules of the game. He must not stoop to anything unfair or unsportsmanlike in order to win.

You may say, well, those things can all be taught the boy in the classroom. Experience will show that preaching in a case like this does not produce the desired results. The boy has to go out on the athletic field or on the debating platform, if you will, and compete, actually compete, in order to acquire these things.

What is education? Well, education helps the young man discipline his mind; it informs his mind and helps him to develop intellectual power; but, I think one thing that we generally lose sight of is the fact that a high school or college should help the young fellow to find himself in every sense of the word, and I believe that the athletic field is the laboratory of experiment which does help the average young fellow find himself.

It is on the athletic field that he experiments with himself, phys-ically, mentally and emotionally. I have never yet seen a high school or college athlete who was not intensely loyal. Loyalty, in my opinion, is one of the finest words in the dictionary. There are so many men who lack that.

On the athletic field they find their possibilities, they learn their limitations, they develop self-restraint, they develop patience and resolution; they develop a sense of fair play and confidence, and they develop the will to win.

Some of you may say, this will to win is a bad thing. In what way is it a bad thing? Education is supposed to prepare a young man for life. Life is competition. Success in life goes only to the man who competes successfully. A successful lawyer is the man who goes out and wins—wins law cases. A successful physician is a man who goes out and wins—saves lives and restores men to health. A successful sales manager is a man who goes out and wins—sells the goods. The successful executive is the man who can make money and stay out of the bankruptcy court. There is no reward for the loser. There is nothing wrong with the will to win. The only penalty should be that the man who wins unfairly should be set down.

I do believe that athletics, properly controlled, supervised, and developed, is an integral part of education, and does do its part in educating young men for life.

The Disappointed Angler

A true story from the Edinburgh Angling Club

The incident which suggested the following song occurred in the autumn of 1851. The day had proved very unpropitious, not a fish having been killed, although several rods had been busy on the water from an early hour of the morning. The party at the "Nest" had finished their second jug after dinner, and the gloamin'—that witching hour for anglers as well as lovers—was fast coming on, when one of the party resolved to have another cast in the "Trows" —a favourite pool or succession of pools—before the sun went down. Near the foot of the "Trows," at a place called the "Brander," a large fish, after the second or third throw, rose to the fly, but missed it. Although the cast was repeated several times, the fish would not stir again, and darkness ultimately drove our angler from the river, but not before he had resolved on another trial after he and the fish had had a night's rest. The fact of a fish having shown itself in the "Brander" could not be concealed from the rest of the party. Our angler reached the "Trows" next morning by six o'clock, having driven from Clovenford, where he was residing, a distance of nearly three miles; but he was just in time to see his anticipated prey stretched on the rocks by the skilful hand of a brother Angler, whose "earlier flee" had wiled the "scaly buffer" from the depths of the "Brander." The temper of even a less enthusiastic fisher might have been ruffled by the disappointment, but he bore it with his accustomed equanimity. The fish weighed 14 lbs., and was in excellent condition.

" 'Twas on a summer afternoon,
A wee before the sun gaed doun,"
That to the "Trows" I wandered doun,
    In hopes to catch a saumon;
I threw my line across the stream,
    Which glittered in the evening beam,
When to my fly, wi' sudden gleam,
    Arose a sonsy saumon.

I started back wi' strange delight,
    For, oh! it was a wondrous sight;
Its size so big—it shone so bright—
    It was a dainty saumon.
I fished it o'er and o'er again,
    Till back and arms did ache wi' pain;
But no! it wadna come again,
    The stupid, senseless saumon!

The day had faded in the west,
    So hame I trudged to tak' my rest,
Nor stopt to pree aught at the "Nest"—
    Resolved to pree that saumon.
But first I marked where it did lie,
    Then upwards gazing at the sky,
I vowed next morn that it should die,
    If ever died a saumon.

I dreamt a' nicht 'bout rod and reel,
    My book o' flees, my fishin'-creel,
An otter, too, that cam' to steal
    Awa' my bonnie saumon.
The sun had tinged the eastern sky,
    When frae my bed, light as a fly,
I rose, my skill again to try,
    And catch that wily saumon.

I reached the "Trows," but oh, the shock!
    My heart beat quick, my knees did knock,
For clots o' blood lay on that rock,
    The blood o' my poor saumon.

Noo, Anglers a', be warn'd by me,
    When next a fish you chance to see,
Tell not a frien', whae'er he be,
    Keep your secret and your saumon.

The Retirement

Addressed to Izaak Walton and all other fishermen

I.

FAREWELL, thou busy world ! and may
    We never meet again :
Here I can eat, and sleep, and pray,
And do more good in one short day,
Than he, who his whole age outwears
Upon the most conspicuous theatres,
Where naught but vanity and vice do reign.

II.

Good God ! how sweet are all things here !
How beautiful the fields appear !
    How cleanly do we feed and lie !
Lord ! what good hours do we keep !
How quietly we sleep !
    What peace ! what unanimity !
How innocent from the lewd fashion
Is all our business, all our recreation !

III.

O how happy here 's our leisure !
O how innocent our pleasure !
O ye valleys !   O ye mountains !
O ye groves, and crystal fountains !
How I love at liberty,
By turns, to come and visit ye !

IV.

Dear Solitude, the soul's best friend,
    That man acquainted with himself dost make,
And all his Maker's wonders to entend,
With thee I here converse at will,
And would be glad to do so still ;
    For it is thou alone that keep'st the soul awake.

V.

How calm and quiet a delight
    Is it alone
To read, and meditate, and write ;
    By none offended, and offending none !
To walk, ride, sit, or sleep at one's own ease,
And, pleasing a man's self, none other to displease !

The Mission of Sport

by Grover Cleveland

While it is most agreeable thus to consider hunting and fishing as constituting, for those especially endowed for their enjoyment, the most tempting of outdoor sports, it is easily apparent that there is a practical value to these sports as well as all other outdoor recreations, which rests upon a broader foundation. Though the delightful and passionate love for outdoor sports and recreation is not bestowed upon every one as a natural gift, they are so palpably related to health and vigor, and so inseparably connected with the work of life and comfort of existence, that it is happily ordained that a desire or a willingness for their enjoyment may be cultivated to an extent sufficient to meet the requirements of health and self-care. In other words, all but the absolutely indifferent can be made to realize that outdoor air and activity, intimacy with nature and acquaintanceship with birds and animals and fish, are essential to physical and mental strength, under the exactions of an unescapable decree.

Men may accumulate wealth in neglect of the law of recreation; but how infinitely much they will forfeit, in the deprivation of wholesome vigor, in the loss of the placid fitness for the quiet joys and comforts of advancing years, and in the displacement of contented age by the demon of querulous and premature decrepitude!

"For the good God who loveth us
He made and loveth all."

Men, in disobedience of this law, may achieve triumph in the world of science, education and art; but how unsatisfying are the rewards thus gained if they hasten the night when no man can work, and if the later hours of life are haunted by futile regrets for what is still left undone, that might have been done if there had been closer communion with nature's visible forms!

In addition to the delight which outdoor recreations afford to those instinctively in harmony with their enjoyment, and after a recognition of the fact that a knowledge of their nerve- and muscle-saving ministrations may be sensibly cultivated, there still remains another large item that should be placed to their credit. Every individual, as a unit in the scheme of civilized social life, owes to every man, woman and child within such relationship an uninterrupted contribution to the fund of enlivening and pleasurable social intercourse. None of us can deny this obligation; and none of us can discharge it as we ought, if our contributions are made in the questionable coin of sordidness and nature's perversion. Our experience and observation supply abundant proof that those who contribute most generously to the exhilaration and charm of social intercourse will be found among the disciples of outdoor recreation, who are in touch with nature and have thus kept fresh and unperverted a simple love of humanity's best environment.

A CHANCE IN THE OPEN FOR ALL

It seems to me that thoughtful men should not be accused of exaggerated fears when they deprecate the wealth-mad rush and struggle of American life and the consequent neglect of outdoor recreation, with the impairment of that mental and physical vigor absolutely essential to our national welfare, and so abundantly promised to those who gratefully recognize, in nature's adjustment to the wants of man, the care of "the good God" who "made and loveth all."

Manifestly, if outdoor recreations are important to the individual and to the nation, and if there is danger of their neglect, every instrumentality should be heartily encouraged which aims to create and stimulate their indulgence in every form.

Fortunately, the field is broad and furnishes a choice for all except those wilfully at fault. The sky and sun above the head, the soil beneath the feet, and outdoor air on every side are the indispensable requisites.

IN THE HAUNTS OF BREAM AND BASS

by Maurice Thompson

DREAMS come true and everything
Is fresh and lusty in the spring.

In groves, that smell like ambergris,
Wind-songs, bird-songs never cease.

Go with me down by the stream,
Haunt of bass and purple bream;

Feel the pleasure, keen and sweet,
When the cool waves lap your feet;

Catch the breath of moss and mold,
Hear the grosbeak's whistle bold;

See the heron all alone
Mid-stream on a slippery stone,

Or, on some decaying log,
Spearing snail or water-frog,

Whilst the sprawling turtles swim
In the eddies cool and dim!

II.

The busy nut-hatch climbs his tree,
Around the great bole spirally,

Peeping into wrinkles gray,
Under ruffled lichens gay,

Lazily piping one sharp note
From his silver-mailed throat,

And down the wind the cat-bird's song
A slender medley trails along.

Here a grackle chirping low,
There a crested vireo;

Every tongue of Nature sings,
The air is palpitant with wings!

Halcyon prophesies come to pass
In the haunts of bream and bass.

Bubble, bubble flows the stream,
Like an old tune through a dream.

Now I cast my silken line;
See the gay lure spin and shine—

While, with delicate touch, I feel
The gentle pulses of the reel.

Halcyon laughs and cuckoo cries,
Through its leaves the plane-tree sighs.

Bubble, bubble flows the stream,
Here a glow and there a gleam,

Coolness all about me creeping,
Fragrance all my senses steeping,

Spice-wood, sweet-gum, sassafras,
Calamus and water-grass,

Giving up their pungent smells
Drawn from Nature's secret wells;

On the cool breath of the morn
Fragrance of the cockspur thorn.

IV.

I see the morning-glory's curl,
The curious star-flower's pointed whorl.

Hear the woodpecker, rap-a-tap!
See him with his cardinal's cap!

And the querulous, leering jay,
How he clamors for a fray!

Patiently I draw and cast,
Keenly expectant, till, at last,

Comes a flash, down in the stream,
Never made by perch or bream,

Then a mighty weight I feel,
Sings the line and whirs the reel!

V.

Out of a gaint tulip-tree,
A great gay blossom falls on me;

Old gold and fire its petals are,
It flashes like a falling star.

A big blue heron flying by
Looks at me with a greedy eye.

I see a striped squirrel shoot
Into a hallow maple-root;

A bumble-bee, with mail all rust,
His thighs puffed out with anther-dust

Clasps a shrinking bloom about,
And draws her amber sweetness out.

Bubble, bubble flows the stream,
Like an old tune through a dream!

A white-faced hornet hurtles by,
Lags a turquoise butterfly,

One intent on prey and treasure,
One afloat on tides of pleasure!

Sunshine arrows, swift and keen,
Pierce the maple's helmet green.

VI

I follow where my victim leads,
Through tangles of rank water-weeds,

O'er stone and root and knotty log,
And faithless bits of reedy bog.

I wonder will he ever stop?
The reel hums like a humming-top!

A thin sandpiper, wild with fright,
Goes into ecstasies of flight,

Whilst I, all flushed and breathless, tear
Through lady-fern and maiden's-hair,

And in my straining fingers feel
The throbbing of the rod and reel!

Bubble, bubble flows the stream,
Like an old tune through a dream!

VII

At last he tires, I reel him in;
I see the glint of scale and fin.

I raise the rod—I shorten line
And safely land him; he is mine!

The belted halcyon laughs, the wren
Comes twittering from its bushy den,

The turtle sprawls upon the log,
I hear the booming of a frog.

Liquid amber's keen perfume,
Sweet-punk, calamus, tulip-bloom,

Glimpses of a cloudless sky
Soothe me as I resting lie.

Bubble, bubble flows the stream,
Like low music through a dream.

HUMOR

High-handed Outrage at Utica

This little story by Artemus Ward, a favorite humorist of the day, was read to his cabinet by Abraham Lincoln before the meeting in which he read the Emancipation Proclamation.

In the Faul of 1856, I showed my show in Utiky, a trooly grate sitty in the State of New York.

The people gave me a cordyal recepshun. The press was loud in her prases.

1 day as I was givin a descripshun of my Beests and Snaiks in my usual flowry stile what was my skorn & disgust to see a big burly feller walk up to the cage containin my wax figgers of the Lord's Last Supper, and cease Judas Iscarrot by the feet and drag him out on the ground. He then commenced fur to pound him as hard as he cood.

"What under the son are you abowt?" cried I.

Sez he, "What did you bring this pussylanermus cuss here fur?" & he hit the wax figger another tremenjis blow on the hed.

Sez I, "You egrejus ass, that air's a wax figger — a representashun of the false 'Postle."

Sez he, "That's all very well fur you to say but I tell you, old man, that Judas Iscarrot can't show hisself in Utiky with impunerty by a darn site!" with which observashun he kaved in Judassis hed. The young man belonged to 1 of the first famerlies in Utiky. I sood him, and the Joory brawt in a verdick of Arson in the 3d degree.

THE O'LINCOLN FAMILY

by WILSON FLAGG

A flock of merry singing-birds were sporting in the grove;
Some were warbling cheerily, and some were making love:
There were Bobolincon, Wadolincon, Winterseeble, Conquedle,—
A livelier set was never led by tabor, pipe, or fiddle,—
Crying, "Phew, shew, Wadolincon, see, see, Bobolincon,
Down among the tickletops, hiding in the buttercups!
I know the saucy chap, I see his shining cap
Bobbing in the clover there—see, see, see!"

Up flies Bobolincon, perching on an apple-tree,
Startled by his rival's song, quickened by his raillery,
Soon he spies the rogue afloat, curveting in the air,
And merrily he turns about, and warns him to beware!
" 'T is you that would a-wooing go, down among the rushes O!
But wait a week, till flowers are cheery,—wait a week, and ere
    you marry,
Be sure of a house wherein to tarry!
Wadolink, Whiskodink, Tom Denny, wait, wait, wait!"

Every one's a funny fellow; every one's a little mellow;
Follow, follow, follow, follow, o'er the hill and in the hollow!
Merrily, merrily, there they hie; now they rise and now they fly;
They cross and turn, and in and out, and down in the middle, and
    wheel about,—
With a "Phew, shew, Wadolincon! listen to me, Bobolincon!—
Happy's the wooing that's speedily doing, that's speedily doing,
That's merry and over with the bloom of the clover!
Bobolincon, Wadolincon, Winterseeble, follow, follow me!"

The Wonderful Adventures
of Alibi Ike

A Ring Lardner Short Story

It rained down in Cincinnati one day and somebody organized a little game o' cards. They was shy two men to make six and ast I and Carey to play.

"I'm with you if you get Ike and make it seven-handed," says Carey.

So they got a hold of Ike and we went up to Smitty's room.

"I pretty near forgot how many you deal," says Ike. "It's been a long wile since I played."

I and Carey give each other the wink, and sure enough, he was just as ig'orant about poker as billiards. About the second hand, the pot was opened two or three ahead of him, and they was three in when it come his turn. It cost a buck, and he throwed in two.

"It's raised, boys," somebody says.

"Gosh, that's right, I did raise it," says Ike.

"Take out a buck if you didn't mean to tilt her," says Carey.

"No," says Ike, "I'll leave it go."

Well, it was raised back at him and then he made another mistake and raised again. They was only three left in when the draw come. Smitty'd opened with a pair o' kings and he didn't help 'em. Ike stood pat. The guy that'd raised him back was flushin' and he didn't fill. So Smitty checked and Ike bet and didn't get no call. He tossed his hand away, but I grabbed it and give it a look. He had king, queen, jack and two tens. Alibi Ike he must have seen me peekin', for he leaned over and whispered to me.

"I overlooked my hand," he says. "I thought all the wile it was a straight."

"Yes," I says, "that's why you raised twice by mistake."

They was another pot that he come into with tens and fours. It was tilted a couple o' times and two o' the strong fellas drawed ahead of Ike. They each drawed one. So Ike throwed away his little pair and come out with four tens. And they was four treys against him. Carey'd looked at Ike's discards and then he says:

"This lucky bum busted two pair."

"No, no, I didn't," says Ike.

"Yes, yes, you did," says Carey, and showed us the two fours.

"What do you know about that?" says Ike. "I'd of swore one was a five spot."

Well, we hadn't had no pay day yet, and after a wile everybody except Ike was goin' shy. I could see him gettin' restless and I was wonderin' how he'd make the get-away. He tried two or three times. "I got to buy some collars before supper," he says.

"No hurry," says Smitty. "The stores here keeps open all night in April."

After a minute he opened up again.

"My uncle out in Nebraska ain't expected to live," he says. "I ought to send a telegram."

"Would that save him?" says Carey.

"No, it sure wouldn't," says Ike, "but I ought to leave my old man know where I'm at."

"When did you hear about your uncle?" says Carey.

"Just this mornin'," says Ike.

"Who told you?" ast Carey.

"I got a wire from my old man," says Ike.

"Well," says Carey, "your old man knows you're still here yet this afternoon if you was here this mornin'. Trains leavin' Cincinnati in the middle o' the day don't carry no ball clubs."

"Yes," says Ike, "that's true. But he don't know where I'm goin' to be next week."

"Ain't he got no schedule?" ast Carey.

"I sent him one openin' day," says Ike, "but it takes mail a long time to get to Idaho."

"I thought your old man lived in Kansas City," says Carey.

"He does when he's home," says Ike.

"But now," says Carey, "I s'pose he's went to Idaho so as he can be near your sick uncle in Nebraska."

"He's visitin' my other uncle in Idaho."

"Then how does he keep posted about your sick uncle?" ast Carey.

"He don't," says Ike. "He don't even know my other uncle's sick. That's why I ought to wire and tell him."

"Good night!" says Carey.

"What town in Idaho is your old man at?" I says.

Ike thought it over.

"No town at all," he says. "But he's near a town."

"Near what town?" I says.

"Yuma," says Ike.

Well, by this time he'd lost two or three pots and he was desperate. We was playin' just as fast as we could, because we seen we couldn't hold him much longer. But he was tryin' so hard to frame an escape that he couldn't pay no attention to the cards, and it looked like we'd get his whole pile away from him if we could make him stick.

The telephone saved him. The minute it begun to ring, five of us jumped for it. But Ike was there first.

"Yes," he says, answerin' it. "This is him. I'll come right down."

And he slammed up the receiver and beat it out o' the door without even sayin' good-by.

"Smitty'd ought to locked the door," says Carey.

"What did he win?" ast Carey.

We figured it up—sixty-odd bucks.

"And the next time we ask him to play," says Carey, "his fingers will be so stiff he can't hold the cards."

Well, we set around a wile talkin' it over and pretty soon the telephone rung again. Smitty answered it. It was a friend of his'n from Hamilton and he wanted to know why Smitty didn't hurry down. He was the one that had called before and Ike had told him he was Smitty.

"Ike'd ought to split with Smitty's friend," says Carey.

"No," I says, "he'll need all he won. It costs money to buy collars and to send telegrams from Cincinnati to your old man in Texas and keep him posted on the health o' your uncle in Cedar Rapids, D.C."

Ike and His Girl Friend, Dolly

You've saw Cap's wife, o' course. Well, her sister's about twict as good-lookin' as her, and that's goin' some.

Cap took his missus down to St. Louis the second trip and the other one come down from St. Joe to visit her. Her name is Dolly, and some doll is right.

Well, Cap was goin' to take the two sisters to a show and he wanted a beau for Dolly. He left it to her and she picked Ike. He'd hit three on the nose that afternoon—off'n Sallee, too.

They fell for each other the first evenin'. Cap told us how it came off. She begin flatterin' Ike for the star game he'd played and o' course he begin excusin' himself for not doin' better. So she thought he was modest and it went strong with her. And she believed everything he said and that made her solid with him—that and her make-up. They was together every mornin' and evenin' for the five days we was there. In the afternoons Ike played the grandest ball you ever see, hittin' and runnin' the bases like a fool and catchin' everything that stayed in the park.

I told Cap, I says: "You'd ought to keep the doll with us and he'd make Cobb's figures look sick."

But Dolly had to go back to St. Joe and we come home for a long serious.

Well, for the next three weeks Ike had a letter to read every day and he'd set in the clubhouse readin' it till mornin' practice was half over. Cap didn't say nothin' to him, because he was goin' so good. But I and Carey wasted a lot of our time tryin' to get him to own up who the letters was from. Fine chanct!

"What are you readin'?" Carey'd say. "A bill?"

"No," Ike'd say, "not exactly a bill. It's a letter from a fella I used to go to school with."

"High school or college?" I'd ask him.

"College," he'd say.

"What college?" I'd say.

Then he'd stall a wile and then he'd say:

"I didn't go to the college myself, but my friend went there."

"How did it happen you didn't go?" Carey'd ask him.

"Well," he'd say, "they wasn't no colleges near where I lived."

"Didn't you live in Kansas City?" I'd say to him.

One time he'd say he did and another time he didn't. One time he says he lived in Michigan.

"Where at?" says Carey.

"Near Detroit," he says.

"Well," I says, "Detroit's near Ann Arbor and that's where they got the university."

"Yes," says Ike, "they got it there now, but they didn't have it there then."

"I come pretty near goin' to Syracuse," I says, "only they wasn't no railroads runnin' through there in them days."

"Where'd this friend o' yours go to college?" says Carey.

"I forget now," says Ike.

"Was it Carlisle?" ast Carey.

"No," says Ike, "his folks wasn't very well off."

"That's what barred me from Smith," I says.

"I was goin' to tackle Cornell's," says Carey, "but the doctor told me I'd have hay fever if I didn't stay up North."

"Your friend writes long letters," I says.

"Yes," says Ike; "he's tellin' me about a ball player."

"Where does he play?" ast Carey.

"Down in the Texas League—Fort Wayne," says Ike.

"It looks like a girl's writin'," Carey says.

"A girl wrote it," says Ike. "That's my friend's sister, writin' for him."

"Didn't they teach writin' at this here college where he went?" says Carey.

"Sure," Ike says, "they taught writin', but he got his hand cut off in a railroad wreck."

"How long ago?" I says.

"Right after he got out o' college," says Ike.

"Well," I says, 'I should think he'd of learned to write with his left hand by this time."

"It's his left hand that was cut off," says Ike; " and he was left-handed."

"You get a letter every day," says Carey. "They're all the same writin'. Is he tellin' you about a different ball player every time he writes?"

"No," Ike says. "It's the same ball player. He just tells me what he does every day."

"From the size o' the letters, they don't play nothin' but double-headers down there," says Carey.

We figured that Ike spent most of his evenin's answerin' the letters from his "friend's sister," so we kept tryin' to date him up for shows and parties to see how he'd duck out of 'em. He was bugs over spaghetti, so we told him one day that they was goin' to be a big feed of it over to Joe's that night and he was invited.

"How long'll it last?" he says.

"Well," we says, "we're goin' right over there after the game and stay till they close up."

"I can't go," he says, "unless they leave me come home at eight bells."

"Nothin' doin'," says Carey. "Joe'd get sore."

"I can't go then," says Ike.

"Why not?" I ast him.

"Well," he says, "my landlady locks up the house at eight and I left my key home."

"You can come and stay with me," says Carey.

"No," he says, "I can't sleep in a strange bed."

"How do you get along when we're on the road?" says I.

" I don't never sleep the first night anywheres," he says. "After that I'm all right."

"You'll have time to chase home and get your key right after the game," I told him.

"The key ain't home," says Ike. "I lent it to one o' the other fellas and he's went out o' town and took it with him."

"Couldn't you borry another key off'n the landlady?" Carey ast him.

"No," he says, "that's the only one they is."

Well, the day before we started East again, Ike come into the clubhouse all smiles.

"Your birthday?" I ast him.

"No," he says.

"What do you feel so good about?" I says.

"Got a letter from my old man," he says. "My uncle's goin' to get well."

"Is that the one in Nebraska?" says I.

"Not right in Nebraska," says Ike.   "Near there."

But afterwards we got the right dope from Cap. Dolly'd blew in from Missouri and was goin' to make the trip with her sister.

* * *

The Funniest Thing in the World

by JAMES WHITCOMB RILEY

The funniest thing in the world, I know,
Is watchin' the monkeys 'at's in the show!—
Jumpin' an' runnin' an' racin' roun',
'Way up the top o' the pole; nen down!
First they're here, an' nen they're there,
An' ist a'most any an' ever'where!—
Screechin' an' scratchin' wherever they go,
They're the funniest thing in the world, I know!

They're the funniest thing in the world, I think:—
Funny to watch 'em eat an' drink;
Funny to watch 'em a-watchin' us,
An' actin' 'most like grown folks does!—
Funny to watch 'em p'tend to be
Skeerd at their tail 'at they happened to see;—
But the funniest thing in the world they do
Is never to laugh, like me an' you!

Uncle Eph

by Eugene Field

My Uncle Ephraim was a man who did not live in vain,
And yet, why he succeeded so I never could explain.
By nature he was not endowed with wit to a degree,
But folks allowed there nowhere lived a better man than he.
He started poor, but soon got rich; he went to Congress then,
And held that post of honor long against much brainier men;
He never made a famous speech nor did a thing of note,
And yet the praise of Uncle Eph welled up from every throat.

I recollect I never heard him say a bitter word;
He never carried to and fro unpleasant things he heard;
He always doffed his hat and spoke to every one he knew;
He tipped to poor and rich alike a genial "howdy-do";
He kissed the babies, praised their looks, and said, "That child will grow
To be a Daniel Webster or our President, I know!"
His voice was so mellifluous, his smile so full of mirth,
That folks declared he was the best and smartest man on earth!

Now, father was a smarter man, and yet he never won
Such wealth and fame as Uncle Eph, "the deestrick's fav'rite son."
He had "convictions," and he was not loath to speak his mind;
He went his way and said his say as he might be inclined.
Yes, he was brainy; yet his life was hardly a success—
He was too honest and too smart for this vain world, I guess!
At any rate, I wondered he was unsuccessful when
My Uncle Eph, a duller man, was so revered of men!

When Uncle Eph was dying he called me to his bed,
And in a tone of confidence inviolate he said:
"Dear Willyum, ere I seek repose in yonder blissful sphere,
I fain would breathe a secret in your adolescent ear:
Strive not to hew your path through life—it really doesn't pay;
Be sure the salve of flattery soaps all you do and say;
Herein the only royal road to fame and fortune lies:
Put not your trust in vinegar—molasses catches flies!"

MOSTLY FOR MEN

The Long Flight

by W. A. PATTERSON
Chairman of the Board, United Air Lines

Reprinted from United Air Lines' MAINLINER Magazine

LATE AT NIGHT I CAN occasionally hear a propeller aircraft miles away, and the far-off, lonely sound of its engines reminds me of the early mail planes and their pilots.

Air mail pilots were the real pioneers of air transportation. Most of them had learned to fly as U.S. army aviators, but the first World War ended before they entered combat. In the following years, some returned to their civilian occupations, some drifted around the country as "barnstormers" at county fairs, and others became pilots for the Post Office Department.

The Post Office had begun experimenting with air mail service in 1918 and within three years progressed to the point of inaugurating day-and-night transcontinental flights. It was an extremely bold step, considering the war-surplus aircraft that was used, the makeshift landing fields, and the utter lack of adequate equipment for communications and navigation.

Each time an air mail pilot left the ground, it was a venture into the unknown. He was wholly dependent on his skill and fortitude, the regular beat of a cumbersome water-cooled engine, and the vicious whims of weather. There were no meteorologists to tell him of conditions ahead—of landing fields obscured by fog or snow; no radio messages to inform him of storm fronts dripping across his path; no electronic devices to guide him to destination.

Pilots had courage, as I've indicated, and they were able to get the mail through in spite of many hazards. After several years of their gallant striving, people who doubted that air transportation would ever become practical began to admit that it was within the realm of human accomplishment.

In the mid-1920's Congress decided that further development of a nation-wide air transport system should rest with the energies and initiative of private enterprise. It was a wise decision. The Kelly Bill of 1925 authorized the Postmaster General to award air mail contracts on the basis of competitive bids. This legislation stimulated the organization of various air transport companies.

Successful bidders on air mail routes went into business in 1926 and the immediate following years, hiring the men who had flown for the Post Office. Thus, the airlines began operations with a seasoned force of pilots, but planes were still deficient in navigation aids and safety devices. It was just as well that passengers were very rare at the outset and mail was the all-important payload.

Present technological development makes it hard to realize the extent to which airlines have advanced the art of flying. Perhaps, I can sum it up by reminding that about 50 years ago the Appalachian Mountains were regarded as an insurmountable barrier that would prevent a transcontinental air system from ever being established.

Time has not eclipsed the achievement of Col. Charles A. Lindbergh in flying the Atlantic in the spring of 1927, but the impetus he gave to air transportation is fading from the memory of many. More than any other one person, he convinced the public that air travel could be as reliable as any form of surface transportation.

When "Slim" returned from Europe, he took it upon himself to visit almost 100 cities across the nation. He flew from place to place day after day, adhering to an exhaustive itinerary. His tour aroused municipal authorities to the need for airport facilities and, incidentally, made it clear to millions that airplanes were capable of maintaining schedule reliability.

Lindbergh was responsible for a nationwide surge of interest in aviation and air transportation. He heads my list of those who deserve more than modest credit for their share in stimulating early development of the industry.

Others in that category include William E. Boeing, founder of the Boeing Airplane Company; Vern Gorst, pioneer airline

operator along the Pacific Coast; Walter T. Varney of Varney Air Lines; P. G. Johnson, whom I succeeded as president of United when it became an independent operating company in 1934; Donald Douglas, Sr., of the aircraft company of that name; and Thorp Hiscock, a onetime banker and rancher who became associated with Boeing Air Transport.

Thorp Hiscock typified the hard-driving men of action who were drawn by the challenge that air transportation offered in early years. They were not afraid to fail. They barged into unknown areas with great confidence, and a surprising number of times, they managed to do what others had not been able to do.

Thorp had never received formal training in engineering or physics, but he made up for it with inventive insights and the ability to stay with a problem until it was whipped. Using trial and error, for example, he and his assistant, William Lawrenz, hit upon a satisfactory system of two-way plane-and-ground radio communications. Expert technicians had tried to achieve this, but they had been balked by engine spark plug interference and other electrical disturbances.

I recall having lunch with Thorp at a Chicago hotel. Throughout the meal he stared into space, apparently lost in thought until suddenly he said, "That's the answer."

He indicated a pennant, which I glimpsed through the window. Freezing rain the night before had soaked the cloth and it had frozen stiff. During luncheon the wind had picked up and the pennant was beginning to flap around, breaking off pieces of ice.

In this trivial event, Thorp had seen a way to develop aircraft de-icers. For a week he busied himself with rubber tubes, expanding and contracting them with air pressure. This was the basic principle subsequently used on de-icer boots attached to the leading edge of aircraft wings. Until this innovation, one of the greatest hazards to flying had been the formation of ice on airplane wings, which interrupted the air flow and caused crashes.

The wildest ride I've ever had on a plane came when Thorp invited me to fly on a Boeing 247, which we were using for experimental purposes. He and his assistant, Fred Hambrick, had been testing two auto-pilot devices. Each "black box" was deficient in their estimation and they concluded they could built a better one by using parts from both.

After we reached altitude, Thorp switched on the improvised autopilot. The plane continued to fly but in very erratic fashion. It behaved somewhat like a roller coaster, except for extremely disconcerting lateral movements. After we landed, Thorp seemed pleased with the test.

"There are still some bugs, but it's a big improvement," he said.

I'm not sure of what had been improved.

We were obliged in those days to rely on our own resourcefulness in finding answers to problems, some without precedent. We made mistakes, many mistakes, but we learned from each experience and managed to move ahead with a little more skill, a little more knowledge.

The airlines at first appeared to offer a negligible market for manufacturers who had the technicians and research facilities to help us advance. In the mid-Thirties, however, some corporations began to realize the growth potential. Engineers were assigned to investigate our requirements and from there on we received valuable cooperation.

In this period there was also a shift in the kind of person drawn to air transportation. We began attracting young people who had taken whatever colleges could offer as preparation for airline careers. In contrast with old timers who had experience but lacked formal educations, the newcomers had formal educations but lacked experience. They complemented each other and this had its benefits.

Pilots, proud of their ability to fly by feel and intuition, began to find strange, new instruments in the cockpit. They were instructed to rely on instruments rather than personal judgment and found this hard to do. They clung to techniques that had served them in the air mail days and, sadly but necessarily, they had to yield their place to pilots who flew by instrument.

Progress aside, we are still in one sense exactly where we began. Jets are marvels of sophisticated engineering but, just as in the days of unpressurized piston-engine planes, we continue wholly dependent on the performance of our personnel. Their knowledge and experience are all-important. Consequently, United's investment in personnel training has risen steadily until it now exceeds $11 million annually—one of our worthiest expenditures.

In looking back to the day in 1929 when I joined Boeing Air Transport, it would be pleasant to play the role of prophet, and say that I knew the airline industry would grow to what it is today. But I cannot honestly say that I anticipated anything like the speed and comfort that jet travel now provides, nor did I expect to see the time when United would carry more than 17 million passengers yearly.

And I never visualized the extent to which air transportation would imbed itself in our national life. I did not foresee that it would become one of the forces that set the pace of an industrialized, urbanized society far different from the

America of four decades ago and in some respects removed from it by a thousand years.

Our ambitions for air travel seemed large scale but they were modest when compared with today's reality. We were building something greater than we realized—something great enough to serve a great nation.

Hawaiian-born William A. Patterson, who recently retired as United's chairman of the board, has guided the destiny of the nation's largest air carrier for more than 32 years. Along the way, he has forged a reputation as one of the true giants in one of the most dynamic industries the world has seen.

A Page from the Poor Richard's Series of Almanacks

Mary's mouth costs her nothing, for she never opens it but at others' expence.

A Doubtful Meaning

The female kind is counted ill:
And is indeed: the contrary;
No man can find: that hurt they will:
But every where: shew charity:
To nobody; malicious still;
In word or deed: believe you me.

He that is of Opinion Money will do every Thing, may well be suspected of doing every Thing for Money.

A rich rogue is like a fat hog,
Who never does good till as dead as a log.

He does not possess wealth, it possesses him.

He that falls in love with himself, will have no rivals.

Women are books, and men the readers be,
Who sometimes in those books erratas see;
Yet oft the reader's raptured with each line,
Fair print and paper, fraught with sense divine;
Tho' some, neglectful, seldom to read,
And faithful wives no more than bibles heed.
Are women books? says Hodge, then would mine were
An Almanack, to change her every year.

The cunning man steals a horse, the wise man lets him alone.

Onions can make ev'n heirs and widows weep.

Necessity has no law; I know some attorneys of the same.

The Days of the '49ers

An interesting description of the camps of '49 is afforded by Dr. J. B. Stillman's "Seeking the Golden Fleece." He says there was "no government, no law;" but "more intelligence and good feeling than in any country I ever saw. . . . Men are valued for what they are. . . . One feels that he has a standing here that it takes a man until he is old and rich to enjoy at home." This ignores the camp-laws, as unauthorized, but tacitly acknowledges the good order and peacefulness prevalent in the mining-region. On the subject of miners' generosity, Mr. Bacon, now an Idaho journalist, and an old California miner, writes me as follows:—

> "I have never lived in any community where there was less crime, or where people were more charitable, than they were in the early mining-camps of California. No one was ever allowed to suffer for necessaries of life, and nowhere were the sick neglected. I remember many instances where a miner with a broken constitution, who had become discouraged or unable to work, and desired to return to his family, was sent home by the miners, and, in addition, was given one or two thousand dollars for a 'home-stake.'"

Theodore Winthrop, that bright, generous poet and novelist, saw the same characteristics in the hearty pioneers of the Pacific Coast, and rejoiced over "the rough sincerity impressed upon people by the life they lead in new countries."

Some of the darker portions of the picture are shown by Theodore J. Johnson, in his "Sights in the Gold-Region;" and his views deserve careful consideration.

> "The thirst for gold, and the labor required to procure it," he says, "overruled all else, and absorbed every faculty. Complete silence reigned among the miners. They addressed not a word to each other for hours."

He says, further, that although enduring great hardships, exposure, and often disease, the miners as a class obtained only a moderate remuneration. The average yield per miner was, he thought, only three or four dollars a day; and not more than one man in a hundred made a fortune, and invested it safely away from the mines. Out of one hundred and twenty men who went around the Horn, and were at the same camps, "not one had great success." These views regarding the average yield of the mines to each toiler are well sustained by the official reports. The five thousand miners of 1848 averaged one thousand dollars apiece, though many of them did not reach the mines till very late in the season; but the hundred thousand miners of 1850 dug out only half as much proportionately, working a longer season, and with far better appliances. The gold-product of the State reached its culmination in 1853, then sinking year after year to a point below the total of 1849, but varying little during the past ten years. The introduction of capital and machinery has rendered it impossible to estimate the amount that each man's labor now produces. The annual gold-yield of the State has been, for a number of years, something over sixteen million dollars; in 1883 it was $16,500,000.

Another very strong statement upon the nature of life in the mines comes from Mr. George F. Parsons, in his Life of Marshall, to which we have previously alluded. He says,—

"It was a mad, furious race for wealth, in which men lost their identity almost, and toiled and wrestled, and lived a fierce, riotous, wearing, fearfully excited life; forgetting home and kindred; abandoning old, steady habits; acquiring all the restlessness, craving for stimulant, unscrupulousness, hardihood, impulsive generosity, and lavish ways, which have puzzled the students of human nature who have undertaken to portray or to analyze that extraordinary period."

He says that a true account of those times would be "so wild, so incredible, so feverish and abnormal," as to remind

one rather of a description of a Walpurgis Night than of an era in real life. In another place we have this graphic picture:—

"Take a sprinkling of sober-eyed, earnest, shrewd, energetic New-England business-men: mingle with them a number of rollicking sailors, a dark band of Australian convicts and cut-throats, a dash of Mexican and frontier desperadoes, a group of hardy backwoodsmen, some professional gamblers, whiskey-dealers, general swindlers, or 'rural agriculturists' as Captain Wragge styles them; and having thrown in a promiscuous crowd of broken-down merchants, disappointed lovers, black sheep, unfledged dry-goods clerks, professional miners from all parts of the world, and Adullamites generally, stir up the mixture, season strongly with gold-fever, bad liquors, faro, monte, rouge-et-noir, quarrels, oaths, pistols, knives, dancing, and digging, and you have something approximating to California society in early days."

Statements such as these concerning the overpowering excitment of the gold-search, and its evil effects, undoubtedly reveal a deep psychical truth. Evil men became more evil, miserly men more miserly, in the Sierra camps. There must have been many to whose souls this "yellow, glittering, precious gold" was a "most operant poison," making "black, white; foul, fair; wrong, right; base, noble;" and over whose wretched lives the spirit of the exiled, ill-starred, manhating Athenian's terrible mockery prevailed in ghastly earnest, until they lived and died in the bitter faith that "this yellow slave" of the exile's scorn could—

"Knit and break religions; bless the accursed;
Make the hoar leprosy adored; place thieves,
And give them title, knee, and approbation
With senators on the bench."

Discovering the Wonders of the Yellowstone Area

by Nathaniel Langford, *Member of the Washburn Expedition*

Montana was organized as a territory on the 26th day of May, 1864, and I continued to reside in that territory until the year 1876, being engaged chiefly in official business of a character which made it necessary, from time to time, for me to visit all portions of the territory. It is a beautiful country. Nature displays her wonders there upon the most magnificent scale. Lofty ranges of mountains, broad and fertile valleys, streams broken into torrents are the scenery of every-day life. These are rendered enjoyable by clear skies, pure atmosphere and invigorating climate.

Ever since the first year of my residence there I had frequently heard rumors of the existence of wonderful phenomena in the region where the Yellowstone, Wind, Snake and other large rivers take their rise, and as often had determined to improve the first opportunity to visit and explore it, but had been deterred by the presence of unusual and insurmountable dangers. It was at that time inhabited only by wild beasts and roving bands of hostile Indians. An occasional trapper or old mountaineer were the only while persons who had ever seen even those portions of it nearest to civilization, previous to the visit of David E. Folsom and C. W. Cook in the year 1869. Of these some had seen one, some another object of interest; but as they were all believed to be romancers their stories were received with great distrust.

The old mountaineers of Montana were generally regarded as great fabricators. I have met with many, but never one who was not fond of practicing upon the credulity of those who listened to the recital of his adventures. James Bridger, the discoverer of Great Salt lake, who had a large experience in wild mountain life, wove so much of romance around his Indian adventures that his narrations were generally received with many grains of allowance by his listeners. Probably no man ever had a more varied and interesting experience during a long period of sojourning on the western plains and in the Rocky Mountains than Bridger, and he did not hesitate, if a favorable occasion offered, to "guy" the unsophisticated. At one time when in camp near "Pumpkin Butte," a well-known landmark near Fort Laramie, rising a thousand feet or more above the surrounding plain, a young attache of the party approached

Mr. Bridger, and in a rather patronizing manner said: "Mr. Bridger, they tell me that you have lived a long time on these plains and in the mountains." Mr. Bridger, pointing toward "Pumpkin Butte," replied: "Young man, you see that butte over there! Well, that mountain *was a hole in the ground* when I came here."

Bridger's long sojourn in the Rocky Mountains commenced as early as the year 1820, and in 1832 we find him a resident partner in the Rocky Mountain Fur Company. He frequently spent periods of time varying from three months to two years, so far removed from any settlement or trading post, that neither flour nor bread stuffs in any form could be obtained, the only available substitute for bread being the various roots found in the Rocky Mountain region.

I first became acquainted with Bridger in the year 1866. He was then employed by a wagon road company, of which I was president, to conduct the emigration from the states to Montana, by way of Fort Laramie, the Big Horn river and Emigrant gulch. He told me in Virginia City, Montana, at that time, of the existence of hot spouting springs in the vicinity of the source of the Yellowstone and Madison rivers, and said that he had seen a column of water as large as his body, spout as high as the flag pole in Virginia City, which was about sixty (60) feet high. The more I pondered upon this statement, the more I was impressed with the probability of its truth. If he had told me of the existence of falls one thousand feet high, I should have considered his story an exaggeration of a phenomenon he had really beheld; but I did not think that his imagination was sufficiently fertile to originate the story of the existence of a spouting geyser, unless he had really seen one, and I therefore was inclined to give credence to his statement, and to believe that such a wonder did really exist.

I was the more disposed to credit his statement, because of what I had previously read in the report of Captain John Mullan, made to the war department. From my present examination of that report, which was made February 14, 1863, and a copy of which I still have in my possession, I find that Captain Mullan says:

"I learned from the Indians, and afterwards confirmed by my own explorations, the fact of the existence of an infinite number of hot springs at the headwaters of the Missouri, Columbia and Yellowstone rivers, and that hot geysers, similar to those of California, exist at the head of the Yellowstone."

The Man Who Sulks

by SAMUEL ELLSWORTH KISER

The world has little pity and few favors to be spent
For the man who is disgruntled and sits sulking in his tent;
If your ventures have not prospered do not idly curse your luck,
But get out and make the people wonder at your manly pluck.

Men will never come to coax you, if you hang back in despair,
To have courage and keep trying to put off the frown you wear;
They will not arrange new chances to replace the ones you lose
While you haunt a gloomy corner clinging to a case of blues.

They are foolishly self-cheated who keep harping on their woes
After they have been defeated, thinking all men are their foes,
And the praise the world is willing to bestow is never meant
For the man who is disgruntled and sits sulking in his tent.

The Characters of Damon Runyon

A living legend in the day of legendary characters

by EDWARD H. WEINER from *The Damon Runyon Story*

To write his stories Runyon merely opened his imagination and let the life of Broadway stroll through. He carefully selected the personalities he desired, dressed them into the characters he needed, supplied all the male members with guns, gave them all appropriate monikers, and allowed them to speak in their native tongue. He appropriated the names of his characters from real life, sometimes, altered others, and invented the rest. His real-life models were often gamblers and gunmen whom any competent New York detective could recognize, and at other times Damon sidetracked law-abiding friends into slightly illegal fictional activities.

Harry the Horse, Little Isadore, and Spanish John are natives of Brooklyn, where they are regarded as disreputable neighbors by the other residents. ". . . many citizens of Brooklyn will be very glad indeed to see Harry the Horse, Little Isadore and Spanish John move away from there," according to the report in one of the stores, "as they are always doing something that is considered a knock to the community, such as robbing people, or maybe shooting or stabbing them, and throwing pineapples, and carrying on generally."

Judge Goldfobber is said to be a "wonderful hand for keeping citizens from getting into the sneezer [jail], and better than Houdini when it comes to getting them out of the sneezer after they are in." Educated Edmund is called Educated Edmund because "he once goes to Erasmus High School and is considered a very fine scholar, indeed . . ." Miss Missouri Martin, who runs the Three Hundred Club, "tells everything she knows as soon as she knows it, which is very often before it happens." Dream Street Rose is a short, thick-set, square-looking old doll, with a square pan and square shoulders, and she's as strong and lively as Jim Londos, the wrestler. "In fact, Jim Londos will never be any better than 6 to 5 in my line over Dream Street Rose, if she is in any kind of shape." Angie the Ox is an importer of fine liquors, besides enjoying a splendid trade in other lines, "including artichokes and extortion."

The Louse Kid has a very weak face, but is supposed to be "a wonderful hand with a burlap bag when anybody wishes to put somebody in such a bag, which is considered a great practical joke in Brooklyn . . ." Rusty Charley is probably the toughest member of the cast, which includes some extremely sturdy individuals. "In fact, this Rusty Charley is what is called a gorilla because he is known to often carry a gun in his pants pocket, and sometimes to shoot people down as dead as door-nails with it if he does not like the way they wear their hats—and Rusty Charley is very critical of hats. The chances are Rusty Charley shoots many a guy in this man's town, and those he does not shoot he sticks with his shiv—which is a knife—and the only reason he is not in jail is because he just gets out of it, and the law does not have time to think up something to put him back in again for."

Regret earned his name because "it seems he wins a very large bet the year the Whitney filly, Regret, grabs the Kentucky Derby, and can never forget it, which is maybe because it is the only very large bet he ever wins in his life." John Wangle is so thin he must be "two pounds lighter than a stack of wheats." One character is called Izzy Cheesecake because he frequents delicatessen stores where he always eats cheesecake. Jo-jo has jowls you can cut steaks off of, and sleepy eyes, and "he sometimes reminds me of an old lion I once seen in a cage in Ringling's circus." There are many more—Sam the Gonoph, Benny South Street, Liverlips, The Brain, Feet Samuels, who has feet like violin cases, Rochester Red, the Pale Face Kid, Big Jule, Hot Horse Herbie, Joe the Joker, a clever dispenser of the hot foot, Frankie Ferocious, an efficient administrator in the murder business, Hymie Banjo Eyes, Dancing Dan, Last Card Louie, Big Nig, and Nick the Greek.

These are the characters who people Runyon's stories. It is obvious that their activities will be stimulating, perhaps vulgar at times, but never conventional or subtle. When a person reads of their crimes in a newspaper, he usually becomes angry at their lawlessness and then disgusted with their misled lives. But in a Runyon story their felonies are magically transformed into amusing adventures; their immorality becomes the spice that brings the high taste of laughter to almost every page. Runyon employs his language like a skilled musician, regulating the pattern of his work carefully so that the tones of comedy and pathos are clear, resonant, and effective.

Runyon's stories brought a new and colorful jargon to the attention of the public. Damon said he had merely recorded the argot he heard along Broadway and was not responsible for any innovations in the American language. In his short-story world all men and women are "guys" and "dolls," a worn-out race horse is described as being "practically mucilage," a doughty individual has "plenty of ticker," a person who owns a grocery store is in the "grocery dodge," a man whose blood pressure is "away up in the paint cards" has high blood pressure, and a "boatrace" is a horse race in which the winner has been dishonestly selected beforehand, while a "tank job" is a prize fight that has been fixed.

Two of the most important nouns in the Runyon stories are "money" and "gun," although these particular words are never used. A gun, either a revolver or an automatic, is a "rod," a "John Roscoe," or an "equalizer." "Equalizer" is the more original and picturesque term, and on every other page of most stories one of the characters "outs with the old equalizer." This usually makes the situation equal in favor of the possessor of the equalizer. Money is referred to as "potatoes" or "scratch." The denominational terms used are a G for a thousand dollars; a "finnif," a "fin," or a "pound note," five dollars; a "deuce," two dollars; and a "buck" or a "bob," one dollar.

.   .   .   .

Life's Formula

How brew the brave drink, Life?
Take of the herb hight morning joy,
Take of the herb hight evening rest,
Pour in pain, lest bliss should cloy,
Shake in sin to give it zest —
Then down with the brave drink, Life!

Author not traced

.   .   .   .

Jean Nicolet — Exceptional Explorer

From *Historic Mackinac* by Edwin O. Wood, LL.D.

Jean Nicolet was a native of Cherbourg, France. He was about thirty-six years old when he undertook this journey to the West, and in him we see one of the earliest of that numerous and picturesque type, the French-Canadian wood rangers, or *coureur de bois*. He had now spent some fifteen years among the Indians learning their manners, customs and habits, and had become thoroughly Indian in his mode of life. He had conducted successfully a mission of peace to the Iroquois, and had sat in the council of the Nipissings, writing down his observations of Indian life. Both by nature and by experience he was well fitted to hold "talks" and smoke the peace pipe with the strange tribes whom it was now determined to cultivate for peace and trade and bring to a knowledge of the true faith.

The course chosen by Nicolet was the old one which Champlain had followed on his first trip to Lake Huron, and which was to become the established route to this region. He visited the Huron villages and met his old Indian friends. The story of his journey, as told by a contemporary, is as follows:

"He embarked in the Huron country, with seven savages; and they passed by many small nations, both going and returning. When they arrived at their destination they fastened two sticks in the earth, and hung gifts thereon, so as to relieve these tribes from the notion of mistaking them for enemies to be massacred. When he was two days' journey from that nation, he sent one of those savages to bear tidings of the peace, which word was specially well received when they heard that it was a European who carried the message; they dispatched several young men to meet the Manitourinon—that is to say 'the wonderful man.' They meet him, they escort him, and carry all his baggage. He wore a grand robe of China damask, all strewn with flowers and birds of many colours. No sooner did they perceive him than the women and children fled, at the sight of a man who carried thunder in both hands—for thus they called the two pistols that he held. The news of his coming quickly spread to the places round about and there assembled four or five thousand men. Each of the chief men made a feast for him, and at one of these banquets they served at least six score beavers. The peace was concluded; he returned to the Hurons, and some time later to the three Rivers, where he continued his employment as Agent and Inspector, to the great satisfaction of both the French and the Indians, by whom he was equally and singularly loved."

Experience

by RALPH WALDO EMERSON

I am thankful for small mercies. I compared notes with one of my friends who expects everything of the universe, and is disappointed when anything is less than the best; and I found that I begin at the other extreme, expecting nothing, and am always full of thanks for moderate goods. . . . In the morning I awake, and find the old world, wife, babes and mother, Concord and Boston, the dear old spiritual world, and even the dear old devil not far off. If we will take the good we find, asking no questions, we shall have heaping measures. The great gifts are not by analysis. Everything good is on the highway.

* * *

Citizen of the World

by JOYCE KILMER From *Trees and Other Poems*

No longer of Him be it said
"He hath no place to lay His head."

In every land a constant lamp
Flames by His small and mighty camp.

There is no strange and distant place
That is not gladdened by His face.

And every nation kneels to hail
The Splendour shining through Its veil.

Cloistered beside the shouting street,
Silent, He calls me to His feet.

Imprisoned for His love of me
He makes my spirit greatly free.

And through my lips that uttered sin
The King of Glory enters in.

Old Poets

by JOYCE KILMER, *from* "TREES AND OTHER POEMS"

If I should live in a forest
  And sleep underneath a tree,
No grove of impudent saplings
  Would make a home for me.

I'd go where the old oaks gather,
  Serene and good and strong,
And they would not sigh and tremble
  And vex me with a song.

The pleasantest sort of poet
  Is the poet who's old and wise,
With an old white beard and wrinkles
  About his kind old eyes.

For these young flippertigibbets
  A-rhyming their hours away
They won't be still like honest men
  And listen to what you say.

The young poet screams forever
  About his sex and his soul;
But the old man listens, and smokes his pipe,
  And polishes its bowl.

There should be a club for poets
  Who have come to seventy year.
They should sit in a great hall drinking
  Red wine and golden beer.

They would shue in of an evening,
  Each one to his cushioned seat,
And there would be mellow talking
  And silence rich and sweet.

There is no peace to be taken
  With poets who are young,
For they worry about the wars to be fought
  And the songs that must be sung.

But the old man knows that he's in his chair
  And that God's on His throne in the sky.
So he sits by the fire in comfort
  And he lets the world spin by.

General Rules of Warfare

Written in the 16th Century by MACHIAVELLI

The same that helps the enemy hurts you: and the same that helps you hurts the enemy.

He who shall be in the war most vigilant to observe the devises of the enemy, and shall take most pain to exercise his army, shall incur least perils and may hope most of victory.

Never lead your men to fight in the field, if first you have not confirmed their minds and know them to be without fear, and to be in good order: for you ought never to enterprise any dangerous thing with your soldiers, except when you see that they have a reasonable chance to win.

It is better to conquer the enemy with famine than with iron.

No purpose is better than that which is hidden from the enemy until you have executed it.

To know in war how to exploit an opportunity helps more than any other thing.

Nature breeds few strong men; industry and exercise make many.

Discipline may do more in war than fury.

When any depart from the enemy's side to come to serve you, when they are faithful, they shall be unto you always a great gain: for the power of the adversaries is more diminished with the loss of those who run away than of those who are slain, although the name of a fugitive is to new friends suspected, to old, odious.

Better it is in selecting the field, to reserve behind the first front aid enough, than to make the front bigger to disperse the soldiers.

He is most difficult to overcome who knows his own power and the same of the enemy.

The courage of the soldiers avails more than the multitude.

Sometimes the situation helps more than courage.

New and sudden things make armies afraid.

Slow and accustomed things are little regarded by them. Therefore, make your army practice and know with small fights a new enemy, before you come to fight in the field with him.

He who with disorder pursues the enemy after he is broken will turn victory into defeat.

He who prepares not necessary victuals to live upon is overcome without iron.

He who trusts more in horsemen than in footmen, or more in footmen than in horsemen, must accommodate himself with the situation.

When you will see if in the day there comes any spy into the camp, cause every man to go to his lodging.

Change purpose when you perceive that the enemy has foreseen it.

Consult with many about those things which you ought to do: the same that you will after do, confer with few.

Soldiers when they abide at home are maintained with fear and punishment; after they are led to war, with hope and with reward.

Good captains come never to fight in the field, except as necessity constrains them and occasion calls them.

In the fight never direct a battle to any other thing than to that for which you have planned it, if you will make no disorder.

The unexpected accidents are remedied with difficulty: those that are anticipated, with ease.

Men, iron, money, and bread are the strength of war, but of these four the first two are most necessary, because men and iron find money and bread, but bread and money find not men and iron.

The unarmed rich man is booty to the poor soldier.

Accustom your soldiers to despise delicate living and lascivious apparel.

This is as much as occurs to me to remind you of, and I know that there might have been said many other things in all of my reasoning, such as how and in how many kinds of ways the antiquity ordered their bands, how they dressed them, and how in many other things they exercised them, and to have joined hereunto many other particulars, which I have not judged necessary, as well because you yourself may see them, as also because my intent has not been to show just how the old service of war was appointed, but how in these days a service of war might be ordained which should have more virtue than the same that is used.

A Worldwide Fellowship

by Dr. Thomas Dooley

Since my earliest days in medical school the work of Doctor Albert Schweitzer has been one of the great inspirations of my life. To enter into correspondence with him was a cause of great satisfaction to me. And the biggest thrill of all occurred recently when I visited the great old gentleman himself. It is difficult to describe him. He has sensitiveness and forcefulness at one and the same time. He is both tender and majestic. His grizzly old face is wonderful to see.

One of Doctor Schweitzer's most important concepts is that of the Fellowship of Those Who Bear the Mark of Pain. I and my men have found this Fellowship wherever we have gone. Who are its members? Doctor Schweitzer believes the members are those who have learned by experience what physical pain and bodily anguish mean. These people, all over the world, are united by a secret bond. He who has been delivered from pain must not think he is now free, at liberty to continue his life and forget his sickness. He is a man whose eyes are opened. He now has a duty to help others in their battles with pain and anguish. He must help to bring to others the deliverance which he himself knows.

Under this Fellowship come not only those who were formerly sick, but those who are related to sufferers, and whom does this not include? On the members of this Fellowship rests the humanitarian task of providing medical help to the "have-nots" of the world. Dr. Schweitzer believes that men of medicine should go forth among the miserable in far off lands and do what has to be done, in the name of God and Man.

* * *

The spirit of man is not a nebulous thing. The spirit of man is this palpable thing in the hearts of Deng and Chai, Earl and Dwight. On this earth each man must find his field of work. . . . Here where the mountains mingle with the night, where there is the anguish of living and dying, here in these high valleys I will work for all my days.

Dr. Thomas Dooley, in reference to his work in Indochina

My Playmates

by Eugene Field

The wind comes whispering to me of the country green and cool—
Of redwing blackbirds chattering beside a reedy pool;
It brings me soothing fancies of the homestead on the hill,
And I hear the thrush's evening song and the robin's morning trill;
So I fall to thinking tenderly of those I used to know
Where the sassafras and snakeroot and checkerberries grow.

What has become of Ezra Marsh, who lived on Baker's hill?
And what's become of Noble Pratt, whose father kept the mill?
And what's become of Lizzie Crum and Anastasia Snell,
And of Roxie Root, who 'tended school in Boston for a spell?
They were the boys and they the girls who shared my youthful play—
They do not answer to my call! My playmates—where are they?

What has become of Levi and his little brother Joe,
Who lived next door to where we lived some forty years ago?
I'd like to see the Newton boys and Quincy Adams Brown,
And Hepsy Hall and Ella Cowles, who spelled the whole school down!
And Gracie Smith, the Cutler boys, Leander Snow, and all
Who I am sure would answer could they only hear my call!

I'd like to see Bill Warner and the Conkey boys again
And talk about the times we used to wish that we were men!
And one—I shall not name her—could I see her gentle face
And hear her girlish treble in this distant, lonely place!
The flowers and hopes of springtime—they perished long ago,
And the garden where they blossomed is white with winter snow.

O cottage near the maples, have you seen those girls and boys
That but a little while ago made, oh! such pleasant noise?
O trees, and hills, and brooks, and lanes, and meadows, do you know
Where I shall find my little friends of forty years ago?
You see I'm old and weary, and I've traveled long and far;
I am looking for my playmates—I wonder where they are!

A Polar Bear Hunt on Fifth Avenue

by W. C. COUP

One of the most exciting and amusing episodes connected with my career as a showman is that which passed into Gotham history as "the bear hunt on Fifth Avenue." And certainly nothing could be more strange and picturesque than a hot chase after a ferocious polar bear along this aristocratic thoroughfare!

In 1873 there were no polar bears in America, and I thought it would be a good stroke of business to obtain some of these beautiful and imposing animals for my menagerie. Therefore I sent an expedition to the Arctic waters to capture a pair. My men finally succeeded in landing two enormous polars in New York. In the process of shifting them from the shipping-box one of these monsters made his escape, and started on a run down the middle of Fifth Avenue. His course was marked by general consternation. Children playing on the streets, seeing an immense white bear lumbering toward them at full speed, screamed and fled in every direction for shelter; horses, frightened at this unusual spectacle, became unmanageable and ran away; nurse-maids, wheeling their small charges, were stricken helpless with terror, and even the street dogs fled howling down the cross streets and into business houses. Everywhere disorder and terror reigned supreme; the streets became suddenly deserted, and one

·would have supposed that a plague had instantly depopulated the city. The police were called out from every adjacent station as soon as it became known that a white bear was loose in the streets of New York. The poor animal, unaccustomed to the strange medley of metropolitan civilization, was more frightened than those who fled before him.

Finally, by the aid of the police and some of the braver citizens, the beast was driven into a basement of a private residence, and there shot. Had the people only realized it, the creature could easily have been captured alive; but fear reigned in every heart, from the child to the policeman, and the latter would not consider anything save instant death to the bear. The animal was very valuable and had cost me a large sum of money, not only for its capture but also for its transportation, and I was exceedingly sorry to lose him in this way. I considered myself exceedingly fortunate, however, to escape as easily as I did, for had the bear done any harm I should have had to pay heavy damages. No person fortunate enough to witness the tumult of that exciting scene can ever forget the bear hunt on Fifth Avenue!

To-morrow Takes Care of To-morrow

by CHARLES SWAIN

Let to-morrow take care of to-morrow,
 Leave things of the future to fate:
What is the use to anticipate sorrow?
 Life's troubles come never too late.
If to hope overmuch be an error,
 Tis one that the wise have preferred;
And how often have hearts been in terror
 Of evils—that never occurred!

* * *

Perfect happiness, I believe, was never intended by the Deity to be the lot of one of His creatures in this world; but that He has very much put in our power the nearness of our approaches to it, is what I have steadfastly believed.

THOMAS JEFFERSON

MAIN STREET

by JOYCE KILMER From *Main Street and Other Poems*

I like to look at the blossomy track of the moon
  upon the sea,
But it isn't half so fine a sight as Main Street used
  to be
When it all was covered over with a couple of
  feet of snow,
And over the crisp and radiant road the ringing
  sleighs would go.

Now, Main Street bordered with autumn leaves,
  it was a pleasant thing,
And its gutters were gay with dandelions early in
  the Spring;
I like to think of it white with frost or dusty in
  the heat,
Because I think it is humaner than any other
  street.

A city street that is busy and wide is ground by a
  thousand wheels,
And a burden of traffic on its breast is all it ever
  feels:
It is dully conscious of weight and speed and of
  work that never ends,
But it cannot be human like Main Street, and
  recognise its friends.

There were only about a hundred teams on Main
  Street in a day,
And twenty or thirty people, I guess, and some
  children out to play.
And there wasn't a wagon or buggy, or a man or
  a girl or a boy
That Main Street didn't remember, and somehow
  seem to enjoy.

The truck and the motor and trolley car and the
  elevated train
They make the weary city street reverberate with
  pain:
But there is yet an echo left deep down within my
  heart
Of the music the Main Street cobblestones made
  beneath a butcher's cart.

God be thanked for the Milky Way that runs
  across the sky,
That's the path that my feet would tread whenever
  I have to die.
Some folks call it a Silver Sword, and some a
  Pearly Crown,
But the only thing I think it is, is Main Street,
  Heaventown.

WHAT IS REVERENCE FOR LIFE?

by ALBERT SCHWEITZER From: *Out of My Life and Thought*

What is Reverence for Life, and how does it arise in us?

If man wishes to reach clear notions about himself and his relation to the world, he must ever again and again be looking away from the manifold, which is the product of his thought and knowledge, and reflect upon the first, the most immediate, and the continually given fact of his own consciousness. Only if he starts from this given fact can he achieve a rational view.

Descartes makes thinking start from the sentence "I think; so I must exist" *(Cogito, ergo sum)*, and with his beginning thus chosen he finds himself irretrievably on the road to the abstract. Out of this empty, artificial act of thinking there can result, of course, nothing which bears on the relation of man to himself, and to the universe. Yet in reality the most immediate act of consciousness has some content. To think means to think something. The most immediate fact of man's consciousness is the assertion: "I am life which wills to live, in the midst of life which wills to live," and it is as will-to-live in the midst of will-to-live that man conceives himself during every moment that he spends in meditating on himself and the world around him.

As in my will-to-live there is ardent desire for further life and for the mysterious exaltation of the will-to-live which we call pleasure, while there is fear of destruction and of that mysterious depreciation of the will-to-live which we call pain: so too are these in the will-to-live around me, whether it can express itself to me, or remains dumb.

Man has now to decide what his relation to his will-to-live shall be. He can deny it. But if he bids his will-to-live change into will-not-to-live, as is done in Indian and indeed in all pessimistic thought, he involves himself in self-contradiction. He raises to the position of his philosophy of life something unnatural, something which is in itself untrue, and which cannot be carried to completion. Indian thought, and Schopenhauer's also, is full of inconsistencies because it cannot help making concessions time after time to the will-to-live, which persists in spite of all negation of the world, though it will not admit that the concessions are really such. Negation of the will-to-live is self-consistent only if it is really willing actually to put an end to physical existence.

If man affirms his will-to-live, he acts naturally and honestly. He confirms an act which has already been accomplished in his instinctive thought by repeating it in his conscious thought. The beginning of thought, a beginning which continually repeats itself, is that man does not simply accept his existence as something given, but experiences it as something unfathomably mysterious. Affirmation of life is the spiritual act by which man ceases to live unreflectively and begins to devote himself to his life with reverence in order to raise it to its true value. To affirm life is to deepen, to make more inward, and to exalt the will-to-live.

At the same time the man who has become a thinking being feels a compulsion to give to every will-to-live the same reverence for life that he gives to his own. He experiences that other life in his own. He accepts as being good: to preserve life, to promote life, to raise to its highest value life which is capable of development; and as being evil: to destroy life, to injure life, to repress life which is capable of development. This is the absolute, fundamental principle of the moral, and it is a necessity of thought.

The great fault of all ethics hitherto has been that they believed themselves to have to deal only with the relations of man to man. In reality, however, the question is what is his attitude to the world and all life that comes within his reach. A man is ethical only when life, as such, is sacred to him, that of plants and animals as that of his fellow men, and when he devotes himself helpfully to all life that is in need of help. Only the universal ethic of the feeling of responsibility in an ever-widening sphere for all that lives — only that ethic can be founded in thought. The ethic of the relation of man to man is not something apart by itself: it is only a particular relation which results from the universal one.

The ethic of Reverence for Life, therefore, comprehends within itself everything that can be described as love, devotion, and sympathy in suffering, joy, or effort.

The world, however, offers us the horrible drama of Will-to-Live divided against itself. One existence holds its own at the cost of another: one destroys another. Only in the thinking man has the Will-to-Live become conscious of other will-to-live, and desirous of solidarily with it. This solidarity, however, he cannot completely bring about, because man is subject to the puzzling and horrible law of being obliged to live at the cost of other life, and to incur again and again the guilt of destroying and injuring life. But as an ethical being he strives to escape whenever possible from this necessity, and as one who has become enlightened and merciful to put a stop to this disunion (Selbstentzweiung) of the Will-to-Live so far as the influence of his own existence reaches. He thirsts to be permitted to preserve his humanity, and to be able to bring to other existences release from their sufferings.

Reverence for Life arising from the Will-to-Live that has become reflective therefore contains affirmation of life and ethics inseparably combined. It aims to create values, and to realize progress of different kinds which shall serve the material, spiritual, and ethical development of men and mankind. While the unthinking modern acceptance of life stumbles about with its ideals of power won by discovery and invention, the acceptance of life based on reason sets up the spiritual and ethical perfecting of mankind as the highest ideal, and an ideal from which alone all other ideals of progress get their real value.

Through ethical acceptance of the world and of life, we reach a power of reflection which enables us to distinguish between what is essential in civilization and what is not. The stupid arrogance of thinking ourselves civilized loses its power over us. We venture to face the truth that with so much progress in knowledge and power true civilization has become not easier but harder. The problem of the mutual relationship between the spiritual and the material dawns upon us. We know that we all have to struggle with circumstances to preserve our humanity, and that we must be anxiously concerned to turn once more toward hope of victory the almost hopeless struggle which many carry on to preserve their humanity amid unfavorable social circumstances.

A deepened, ethical will to progress which springs from thought will lead us back, then, out of uncivilization and its misery to true civilization. Sooner or later there must dawn the true and final Renaissance which will bring peace to the world.

* * * * *

Great books have changed men's lives and altered the current of history.

— WOODROW WILSON

Great Thoughts From Ancient Leaders

by WILLIAM PENN, from *No Cross, No Crown*

Cyrus (than whom a greater Monarch we hardly find in Story) is more famous for his Virtue, than his Power; and indeed it was *that* which gave him Power. God calls him his Shepherd; Now let us see the Principles of his Conduct and Life: So Temperate was he in his Youth, that when Astyages urged him to drink Wine, he answered, "I am afraid lest there should be poison in it; having seen thee reel and sottish after having drunk thereof." And so careful was he to keep the Persians from Corruption of Manners, that he would not suffer them to leave their Rude and Mountainous Country for one more Pleasant and Fruitful, lest, through Plenty and Ease, Luxury at last might debase their Spirits. And so very Chaste was he, that having taken a Lady of Quality, a most Beautiful Woman, his Prisoner, he refused to see her, saying, "I have no mind to be a Captive to my Captive."

It seems, he claimed no such Propriety; but shunned the occasion of Evil. The Comptroller of his Household asking him one day, what he would please to have for his Dinner? "Bread," saith he; "for I intend to Encamp nigh the Water:" A short and easy Bill of Fare: But this shows the power he had over his Appetite, as well as his Soldiers; and that he was fit to Command others, that could Command himself. According to another saying of his, "No man is worthy to Command, who

is not better than those who are to Obey." And when he came to die, he gave this Reason of his Belief of Immortality, "I cannot persuade myself to think that the Soul of man, after having sustained itself in a mortal Body, should perish, when delivered of it, for want of it." A saying of perhaps as great weight, as may be advanced against Atheism from more enlightened Times.

_____

Artaxerxes Mnemon, being upon an extraordinary occasion reduced to Eat Barley Bread and dried Figs, and drink Water; "What Pleasure," saith he, "have I lost till now, through my Delicacies and Excess!"

_____

Agathocles, becoming King of Sicily, from being the Son of a Potter, always to humble his Mind to his Original, would be daily served in some Earthen Vessels upon his Table: an Example of Humility and Plainness.

_____

Philip, King of Macedon, upon three sorts of good News arrived in one day, feared too much success might transport him immoderately; and therefore prayed for some Disappointments to season his Prosperity, and caution his Mind under the Enjoyment of it. He refused to oppress the Greeks with his Garrisons, saying, "I had rather retain them by kindness than fear; and to be always Beloved, than for a while Terrible." One of his Minions persuading him to decline hearing of a Cause, wherein a particular Friend was Interested; "I had much rather," says he, "thy Friend shall lose his Cause, than I my Reputation." Seeing his Son Alexander endeavor to gain the Hearts of the Macedonians by Gifts and Rewards, "Canst thou believe," says he, "that a man that thou hast corrupted to thy Interests will ever be true to them?" When his Court would have had him quarreled and corrected the Peloponnenses for their Ingratitude to him, he said, "By no means, for if they despise and abuse me after being kind to them, what will they do if I do them harm?" A great Example of Patience in a King, and wittily said. Like to this was his reply to the Ambassadors of Athens, whom asking after Audience, if he could do them any Service, and one of them surlily answering, "The best thou canst do us is to hang thyself." He was nothing disturbed, though his Court murmured; but calmly said to the Ambassador, "Those who suffer Injuries are better People than those that do them." To conclude with him, being one day fallen along the ground, and seeing himself in that Posture, cried out, "What a small Spot of Earth do we take up, and yet the whole World cannot content us!"

Ben Franklin's Accumulated Advice

"I stopt my Horse lately where a great Number of people were, collected at a Vendue of Merchant Goods. The Hour of Sale not being come, they were conversing on the Badness of the Times, and one of the Company call'd to a plain clean old Man, with white Locks, 'Pray, Father Abraham, what think you of the Times? Won't these heavy Taxes quite ruin the Country? How shall we be ever able to pay them? What would you advise us to?'— Father Abraham stood up, and reply'd, 'If you'd have my Advice, I'll give it you in short, for a Word to the Wise is enough, and many Words won't fill a Bushel, as Poor Richard says.' They join'd in desiring him to speak his Mind, and gathering round him, he proceeded as follows:

" 'Friends,' says he, 'and neighbours, the Taxes are indeed very heavy, and if those laid on by the Government were the only Ones we had to pay, we might more easily discharge them; but we have many others, and much more grievous to some of us. We are taxed twice as much by our Idleness, three times as much by our Pride, and four times as much by our Folly, and from these Taxes the Commissioners cannot ease or deliver us by allowing an Abatement. However let us hearken to good Advice, and something may be done for us; God helps them that help themselves, as Poor Richard says in his Almanack of 1733.

" 'It would be thought a hard Government that should tax its People one tenth Part of their Time, to be employed in its Service. But Idleness taxes many of us more more, if we reckon all that is spent in absolute Sloth, or doing of nothing, with that which is spent in idle Employments or Amusements, that amount to nothing. Sloth, by bringing on Diseases absolutely shortens Life. Sloth, like Rust, consumes faster than Labour wears, while the used Key is always bright, as Poor Richard says. But dost thou love Life, then do not squander Time, for that's the Staff Life is made of, as poor Richard says.—How much more than is necessary do we spend in Sleep! forgetting that The Sleeping Fox catches no Poultry, and that there will be sleeping enough in the Grave, as Poor Richard says. If Time be of all Things the most precious, wasting of Time must be, as Poor Richard says, the greatest Prodigality, since, as he elsewhere tells us, Lost Time is never found again; and what we call Time-enough, always proves little enough. Let us then be up and doing, and doing to the Purpose; so by Diligence shall we do more with less Perplexity. Sloth makes all Things difficult, but Industry all Things easy, as Poor Richard says; and He that riseth late, must trot all Day, and shall scarce overtake his Business at night. While Laziness travels so slowly, that Poverty soon overtakes him, as we read in Poor Richard, who adds, Drive thy Business, let that not drive thee; and Early to Bed, and early to rise, makes a Man healthy, wealthy, and wise.

.   .   .   .

" 'So much for Industry, my Friends, and Attention to one's own Business; but to these we must add Frugality, if we would make our Industry more certainly successful. A man may, if he knows not how to save as he gets, Keep his nose all his life to the Grindstone, and die not worth a Groat at last.

.   .   .   .

" 'And now to conclude, Experience keeps a dear School, but Fools will learn in no other, and scarce in that; for it is true, we may give Advice, but we cannot give Conduct, as Poor Richard says: However, remember this, They that won't be counselled, can't be helped, as Poor Richard says: and farther, That if you will not hear Reason, she'll surely wrap your Knuckles.'

"Thus the old Gentleman ended his Harangue. The People heard it, and approved the Doctrine, and immediately practised the contrary, just as if it had been a common Sermon; for the Vendue opened and they began to buy extravagantly, notwithstanding all his Cautions and their own Fear of Taxes."

In School Days

by John Greenleaf Whittier

Still sits the schoolhouse by the road,
  A ragged beggar sunning;
Around it still the sumachs grow,
  And blackberry-vines are running.

Within, the master's desk is seen,
  Deep scarred by raps official;
The warping floor, the battered seats,
  The jack-knife's carved initial;

The charcoal frescoes on its wall;
  Its door's worn sill, betraying
The feet that, creeping slow to school,
  Went storming out to playing!

Long years ago a winter sun
  Shone over it at setting;
Lit up its western window-panes,
  And low eaves' icy fretting.

It touched the tangled golden curls,
  And brown eyes full of grieving,
Of one who still her steps delayed
  When all the school were leaving.

For near her stood the little boy
  Her childish favor singled;
His cap pulled low upon a face
  Where pride and shame were mingled.

Pushing with restless feet the snow
  To right and left, he lingered;—
As restlessly her tiny hands
  The blue-checked apron fingered.

He saw her lift her eyes; he felt
  The soft hand's light caressing,
And heard the tremble of her voice,
  As if a fault confessing.

"I'm sorry that I spelt the word:
  I hate to go above you,
Because,"— the brown eyes lower fell,—
  "Because, you see, I love you!"

Still memory to a gray-haired man
  That sweet child-face is showing.
Dear girl! the grasses on her grave
  Have forty years been growing!

He lives to learn, in life's hard school,
  How few who pass above him
Lament their triumph and his loss,
  Like her,— because they love him.

Theodore Roosevelt, The Ranch Hand

by BILL SEWALL

Roosevelt led the regular life of a Dakota ranchman except that he did a good deal of reading and writing which ranchmen, as a rule, are not such good hands at. He did all of the regular work of the cowboy and used to attend the round-ups that were held within a hundred or two hundred miles of our ranch. For days on end and all day long he would ride the range after the cattle.

In *Wilderness Hunter* he tells about it better than I can.

Early in June, just after the close of the regular spring round-up, a couple of supply-wagons with a score of riders between them were sent to work some hitherto untouched country between the Little Missouri and the Yellowstone. I was going as the representative of our own and one or two other neighboring hands, but as the round-up had halted near my ranch I determined to spend a day there and then to join the wagons, the appointed meeting-place being a cluster of red scoria buttes some forty miles distant, where there was a spring of good water. Most of my day at the ranch was spent in slumber, for I had been several weeks on the round-up, where nobody ever gets quite enough sleep. . . . The men are in the saddle from dawn until dusk, at the time when the days are longest, and in addition there is the regular night guarding and now and then a furious storm or a stampede, when for twenty-four hours at a stretch the riders only dismount to change horses or snach a mouthful of food.

I started in the bright sunrise, riding one horse and driving loose before me eight others, one carrying my bedding. They traveled strung out in single file. . . . In mid-afternoon I reached the wagons. . . . Our wagon was to furnish the night guards for the cattle; and each of us had his gentlest horse tied ready to hand. The night guards went on duty two at a time for two-hour watches. By good luck my watch came last. My comrade was a happy-go-lucky young Texan who for some inscrutable reason was known as "Latigo Strap"; he had just come from the South with a big drove of trail cattle. A few minutes before two one of the guards who had gone on duty at midnight rode into camp and wakened us by shaking our shoulders. . . . One of the annoyances of guarding, at least in thick weather, is the occasional difficulty of finding the herd after leaving camp, or in returning to camp after the watch

is over; there are few things more exasperating than to be helplessly wandering about in the dark under such circumstances. However, on this occasion there was no such trouble, for it was a brilliant starlit night and the herd had been bedded down by a sugar-loaf butte which made a good landmark.

As we reached the spot we could make out the forms of the cattle lying close together on the level plain; and then the dim figure of a horseman rose vaguely from the darkness and moved by in silence; it was the other of the two midnight guards on his way back to his broken slumber. At once we began to ride slowly round the cattle in opposite directions. We were silent, for the night was clear and the herd quiet.

In wild weather, when the cattle are restless, the cowboys never cease calling and singing as they circle them, for the sounds seem to quiet the beasts. For over an hour we steadily paced the endless round. Then faint streaks of gray appeared in the east. Latigo Strap began to call merrily to the cattle. A coyote came sneaking over the butte and halted to yell and wail. As it grew lighter the cattle became restless, rising and stretching themselves, while we continued to ride around them.

"Then the bronc' began to pitch
And I began to ride;
He bucked me off a cut bank.
Hell! I nearly died!"

sang Latigo from the other side of the herd. A yell from the
wagons afar off told that the cook was summoning the sleeping cow-punchers to breakfast . . . all the cattle got on their
feet and started feeding.

Roosevelt was afraid of nothing and nobody. I remember a
"bad man" he met once in some small town in the Bad Lands.
The man had been drinking and he had heard of Roosevelt,
the new-comer to the frontier. Theodore was not a big man—
he was only of medium height, weighing about a hundred and
fifty pounds, and he wore glasses. But grit to the heel! The
fellow called him a "four-eyed tenderfoot" and tried to take
his measure in abusive language. Theodore paid no attention
to all this, and the tough naturally concluded that he was
afraid of him. Suddenly, Roosevelt let out and caught him on
the butt of the jaw—and he flattened out. This gained him
some reputation.

YOU MAKE YOUR LIFE WHAT IT IS
From Montaigne's *Essays*

If you have made your profit of life, you have had enough
of it, go your way satisfied. . . . If you have not known how to
make the best use of it, and if it was unprofitable for you, what
need you care to lose it, to what end would you desire longer
to keep it? . . . Life in itself is neither good nor evil; it is the
scene of good or evil, as you make it; and if you have lived a
day, you have seen all: one day is equal, and like to all other
days; there is no other light, no other shade: this very sun, this
moon, these very stars, this very order and revolution of things,
is the same your ancestors enjoyed, and that shall also entertain
your posterity.

THE EXCURSION
by WILLIAM WORDSWORTH

I have seen . . .
A curious child, who dwelt upon a tract
Of inland ground, applying to his ear
The convolutions of a smooth-lipped shell;
To which, in silence hushed, his very soul
Listened intensely; and his countenance soon
Brightened with joy; for from within were heard
Murmurings, whereby the monitor expressed
Mysterious union with its native sea.
Even such a shell the universe itself
Is to the ear of Faith; and there are times,
I doubt not, when to you it doth impart
Authentic tidings of invisible things;
Of ebb and flow, and ever-during power;
And central peace, subsisting at the heart
Of endless agitation.

* * * * * * * * * * * * *

A Democracy Cannot Govern An Empire
From Thucydides *Speech by Cleon*

I have observed again and again that a democracy cannot
govern an empire; and never more clearly than now, when I
see you regretting the sentence you pronounced on the Mity-
leneans. Having no fear or suspicion of one another, you deal
with your allies on the same principle. You do not realize that,
whenever you yield to them out of pity, or are prevailed on
by their pleas, you are guilty of a weakness dangerous to yourselves and receive no gratitude from them. You need to bear
in mind that your empire is a *despotism* exercised over unwill-
ing subjects who are ever conspiring against you. They do not
obey because of any kindness you show them: they obey just
so far as you show yourselves their masters. They have no
love for you, but are held down by force. . . .

You must not be misled by pity, or eloquent pleading or
by generosity. There are no three things more fatal to empire.

On A Runaway Circus Train

by W. C. Coup, *from*
SAWDUST AND SPANGLES

I once had a very thrilling experience while riding in the cab of the locomotive pulling our train from Indiana, Pa. This station is on one of the branches of the Pennsylvania Railroad, high up on the mountain, the grade there being exceedingly heavy. It is, I believe, conceded to be one of the steepest grades on that system. There is also a horse-shoe bend, or curve, similar to the well-known one on the main line. While standing on the platform, about the time the last car was being loaded, I was accosted by the engineer, who inquired if I had ever traveled on a locomotive and if I would like to take such a trip. I replied that I would like to do so, and boarded the engine with him. A few moments later the signal bell was rung and we pulled out into the darkness. I placed myself so as not to be in the way of the engineer and fireman and was soon lost in meditation.

The sensation was indescribably weird and thrilling. The scene was shrouded in darkness, and, as we flew along the road, the only discernible objects were the trees, which seemed to me like giant sentinels saluting as we flew past. Now and then we caught glimpses of lights in the mountain valleys, but they passed by like a streak of lightning, so rapidly were we going.

"How far can your practiced eye discern objects on a night like this?" I asked the engineer.

"Only a rod or two," he answered.

"In that case," said I, "you could never stop the train to prevent a collision should an obstruction present itself?"

"No—not with these brakes," he replied.

As he said this his face blanched and he whistled hard for down brakes. Finally I heard him exclaim: "God help us! We're running away!"

On, on we sped down the decline at a speed that was something frightful. The engine rattled and shook, and several times appeared to be almost toppling over. It was impossible to stand, and I held on by the window ledge for dear life. Down the mountain we sped altogether helpless! We had no control over the train, loaded down, as it was, with toppling chariots, with horses, animals, elephants, camels and human freight.

PANIC AMONG THE ANIMALS

Evidently the animals instinctively knew the danger, for above the rattle and roar of the train could occasionally be heard some of those strange trumpetings which proceed from an animal only in moments of danger—often just before a storm or cyclone. Momentarily I expected the whole train to be thrown from the tracks and down the mountain side. By the occasional streaks of light that flew past us I could see the blanched faces of both the engineer and fireman, and knew that they fully realized our awful danger. Both of them, however, kept perfectly cool, and I tried to imitate their example. How far I succeeded I do not know, but I do know that my nerves were strung to a higher pitch than they ever were before.

A blinding rainstorm added to the horror of the situation, and, with the speed at which we were traveling, each drop seemed to have the penetrating power of a shot. Quick as a flash the thought passed through my head: What if we meet a train? Just at that moment we sped past Blairsville at the junction of the branch road and the main line. The station lights seemed mere specks. As we struck the switch the engine jumped and almost left the track. Looking back we could see the rear lights of our train swaying in the path like a ship tempest-tossed at sea. Our speed seemed to increase as we flew along the main line.

We had gone twenty miles when a whistle was heard ahead.

"What is it?" I asked.

"Another train," replied the engineer; "it will pass us now," and as he was speaking the reflecting lights of its engine appeared, apparently not six rods from us. With lightning rapidity the trains passed each other and the "windage," to use a nautical term, nearly took my breath.

During all this time, which positively seemed hours, my thoughts were not of the pleasantest. On, on we dashed, the engine frequently jumping as it struck something on the track. It seemed to me a miracle that the train did not lurch sheer over some one of the terrible embankments. The fireman was not engaged in tending the fire. It was unnecessary. We were all mute spectators of the scene being enacted by this silent machine—the marvelous and likelife invention of man. Gradually, at last, our speed began to slacken. We had reached a grade. The danger was past and our lives were saved!

FAME

by J. B. TABB

Their noon-day never knows
What names immortal are:
'Tis night alone that shows
How star surpasseth star.

SLEEP AND POETRY

by JOHN KEATS

Stop and consider! Life is but a day;
A fragile dewdrop on its perilous way
From a tree's summit; a poor Indian's sleep
While his boat hastens to the monstrous steep
Of Montmorenci,—Why so sad a moan?
Life is the rose's hope while yet unblown;
The reading of an ever-changing tale;
The light uplifting of a maiden's veil;
A pigeon tumbling in clear summer air;
A laughing school-boy, without grief or care,
Riding the springy branches of an elm.

The Women's World

What Am I Without Thee?

by SIDNEY LANIER *from* POEM OUTLINES

What am I without thee, Beloved?
A mere stem, that hath no flower;
A sea forever at storm, without its calms;
A shrine, with the Virgin stolen out;
A cloud void of lightning;
A bleak moor where yearnings moan like the winter
  winds;
A rock on sea-sand, whence the sea harth retired, and
  no longer claspeth and loveth it;
A hollow oak with the heart riven thereout, living by
  the bark alone;
A dark star;
A bird with both wings broken;
A Dryad in a place where no trees are;
A brook that never reacheth the sea;
A mountain without sunrise thereon and without
  springs therein;
A wave that runneth on forever, to no shore;
A raindrop suspended between Heaven and Earth,
  arrested in his course;
A bud, that will never open;
A hope that is always dying;
An eye with no sparkle in it;
A tear wept, dropped in the dust, cold;
A bow whereof the string is snapped;
An orchestra, wanting the violin;
A poor peom;
A bent lance;
A play without plot or denouement;
An arrow, shot with no aim;
Chivalry without his Ladye;
A sound unarticulated;

A water-lily left in a dry lake-bed;
Sleep without a dream and without a waking time;
A pallid lip;
A grave whereafter cometh neither Heaven nor hell;
A broken javelin fixed in a breastplate;
A heart that liveth, but throbbeth not;
An Aurora of the North, dying upon the ice, in the
      night;
A blurred picture;
A lonesome, lonesome, lonesome yearning lover!

. . . .

Take all away from me
But leave me ecstasy,
And I am richer then
Than all my fellow-men.
Is it becoming me
To dwell so wealthily,
When at my very door
Are those possessing more,
In abject poverty?

—EMILY DICKINSON
From *Letters of Emily Dickinson*

. . . .

THE FIRST ARTIST

by JAMES McNEILL WHISTLER

In the beginning, man went forth each day—some to do battle, some to the chase; others, again, to dig and to delve in the field—all that they might gain and live, or lose and die. Until there was found among them one, differing from the rest, whose pursuits attracted him not, and so he staid by the tents with the women, and traced strange devices with a burnt stick upon a gourd.

This man, who took no joy in the ways of his brethren— who cared not for conquest, and fretted in the field—this designer of quaint patterns—this deviser of the beautiful—who perceived in Nature about him curious curvings, as faces are seen in the fire—this dreamer apart, was the first artist. . . .

We have then but to wait—until, with the mark of the gods upon him—there come among us again the chosen—who shall continue what has gone before.

LIFE IS THE COMPOSITE

by JAMES MARTINEAU

The mere lapse of years is not life. To eat, and drink, and sleep,—to be exposed to darkness and the light,—to pace round in the mill of habit, and turn thought into an implement of trade,—this is not life. In all this but a poor fraction of the consciousness of humanity is awakened; and the sanctities will slumber which make it worth while to be. Knowledge, truth, love, beauty, goodness, faith, alone can give vitality to the mechanism of existence. The laugh of mirth that vibrates through the heart; the tears that freshen the dry wastes within; the music that brings childhood back; the prayer that calls the future near; the doubt which makes us meditate; the death which startles us with mystery; the hardship which forces us to struggle; the anxiety that ends in trust; are the true nourishment of our natural being.

"Yours Fraternally"

by EUGENE FIELD

An editor in Kankakee
    Once falling in a burning passion
With a vexatious rival, he
    Wrote him a letter in this fashion:
"You are an ass uncouth and rude,
    And will be one eternally."
Then, in an absent-minded mood,
    He signed it "Yours fraternally."

An Overworked Word

by EUGENE FIELD

We wake up and make up,
    We rake up, we fake up,
And use the word "up" when we can.
    We drink up and think up,
    We kink up and shrink up,
And do up a shirt or a man.

    We slack up or back up,
    We stack up and whack up,
And hold up a man or an ace;
    We beer up and cheer up,
    We steer up and clear up,
And work up ourselves or a case.

    We walk up and talk up,
    We stalk up and chalk up,
And everywhere "up" 's to be heard;
    We wet up and set up,
    But hanged if we let up
On "up," the much overworked word.

DOLLEY MADISON
and the First Inaugural Ball

by ESTHER SINGLETON

Jefferson remained in Washington to take part in the ceremonies of Inauguration of his late Secretary of State. A brief
description of these is given J. Q. Adams:

"I went to the Capitol and witnessed the inauguration of
Mr. Madison as President of the United States. The House was
very much crowded, and its appearance very magnificent. He
made a very short speech, in a tone of voice so low that he
could not be heard, after which the official oath was adminis-
tered to him by the Chief Justice of the United States, the four
other Judges of the Supreme Court being present, and in their
robes. After the ceremony was over, I went to pay the visit of
custom. The company was received at Mr. Madison's house;
he not having yet removed to the President's house. Mr. Jefferson was among the visitors. The Court had adjourned until
two o'clock . . . I came home to dinner, and in the evening went
with the ladies to a ball at Long's in honor of the new President.
The crowd was excessive—the heat oppressive, and the enter-
tainment bad. Mr. Jefferson was there. About midnight the
ball broke up."

According to another account, the "little great man," President Madison attired in a brown suit of cloth, grown from sheep on the Livingston farm, *Clermont* on the Hudson, drove to the Capitol from his house in High Street, Georgetown, escorted by two troops of local cavalry under Capt. Brent. After the ceremonies within the Capitol, the newly-made President went outside, reviewed the military forces and returned to his home. Here he held a reception. The street was full of carriages, and people came in such crowds that many of the guests had to wait half an hour before they could get in. Every room in the house was filled to overflowing; and punch and cake were offered to all. Mr. and Mrs. Madison stood near the door of the drawing-room to receive the guests; she, as usual, the dominating personality. Her costume met with the approval of her fair contemporaries, one of whom described her as looking "beautiful." She wore a plain cambric dress with a very long train, plain round the neck without and kerchief, and a "beautiful bonnet of purple velvet and white satin with white plumes."

It is doubtful if any preceding event had attracted such crowds to Washington. Stage-coaches, for several weeks and days before the Inauguration, had been whirling along the roads from north, south, east, and west, bringing visitors from New England, South Carolina, New York, New Jersey, and Virginia. One tavern-keeper near Washington saw three stage-coaches pass in one day!

Crowded as the Madison reception had been, the first Inaugural Ball brought the visitors out in full force. Every kind of conveyance known to the time and place was represented in front of Long's Hotel on Capitol Hill that night. Stylish private coaches and coaches drawn by mules mingled in democratic fashion with hired carriages and stage-coaches. The Madisons came in their handsome coach drawn by four horses, and with colored coachman and footmen.

Although the admission was by ticket only, these tickets obtainable through the managers, the rooms were so crowded that some of the ladies stood on benches to see the chief figures in the drama make their entrance. The room, too, was so hot that the panes in the windows were smashed in order to give ventilation.

The ball opened at seven o'clock. First the band played *Jefferson's March,* and Mr. Jefferson entered with Mr. Coles. He said to a friend: "Am I too early? You must tell me how to behave, for it is more than forty years since I have been to a ball," Within a few moments the band began to play *Madison's March,* and the President's party entered. Mrs. Madison came first, on the arm of one of the managers, wearing a costume that displayed her beautiful taste. It was a pale buff velvet with a long train, devoid of trimming. Her headdress was sent from Paris and made of the same velvet, trimmed with white satin, and two handsome bird-of-Paradise plumes. A pearl necklace, earrings and bracelets completed this rich dress. The President followed with Mrs. Cutts. He was in black, with ruffles at his throat. His stockings were silk, and his shoes were ornamented with silver buckles. His peculiar springing step, as if he were trying to make himself seem taller than usual, was the only indication he gave of the consciousness that he was the most important personage in the assembly.

The only Diplomats present were Gen. Turreau, the French Minister, David M. Erskine, the British Minister, with his American wife (who was Miss Cadwallader of Philadelphia), and Peter Petersen, the Danish Minister. Mrs. Madison was escorted to supper by the French Minister and Mrs. Cutts by the British. The table was set in the form of a crescent with Mrs. Madison in the centre, with the French and English Ministers on either side, Mrs. Cutts on the right and Mrs. Robert Smith, wife of the Secretary of the Navy, on the left. The President sat opposite Mrs. Madison. Mr. Jefferson remained only two hours, but "seemed in high spirits and his countenance beamed with a benevolent joy." Mr. Madison, on the other hand, "seemed spiritless and exhausted." He and Mrs. Madison left immediately after supper. Music and dancing continued until midnight, when everything stopped.

The most commanding personality in Washington society through four Administrations was undoubtedly Mrs. Madison. We have seen that she had the run of the President's house during Jefferson's occupancy of it, and there she ruled in regal state until its destruction in 1814. All who came in contact with her socially bore witness to her queenly carriage and charming ways. Her diminutive husband was reduced to utter insignificance in comparison with herself on all social occasions. Though she had never been abroad, her natural talents and social tact enabled her to hold her own with Cabinet ladies and those of the Diplomatic Circle who had had experience of Foreign Courts.

The Miracle of the Holy Grail

by FERRIS GREENSLET

King Galahad of Sarras ruled righteously for a year and a day. And upon a hill near his palace he made a sacred place. There was he building a Golden Tree. Each morning and evening he repaired thither to make a prayer to God; and daily he added gold and gems to his tree. So at the year's end the Golden Tree was perfect.

On the morrow went Galahad to it to worship. Then of a sudden there was in that Sacred Place the holy swoon of the Grail; and Sir Galahad, now at the haven of his hope, began to tremble very greatly. Then there came a company of angels, and with them in a white robe Joseph of Arimathea, and high aloft, with a crown of thorns about it, bore he the naked Grail. Then to his knees went Galahad, and crown and sceptre fell from him, and his face upturned in adoration became as the fact of a child.

Now was the soul of Galahad too great in knowledge and power and joy to abide crippled in his earthly body. So he sent for Percival and Bors and kissed them, and thereafter was he never more seen on this earth. And a hand came down from Heaven and took the Grail. And since has there never been a man so hardy as to say that he has seen the Holy Grail.

Christmas Treasures

by EUGENE FIELD

From *A Little Book of Western Verse*, copyrighted, 1889
by EUGENE FIELD, and published by Charles Scribner's Sons

I count my treasures o'er with care,—
   The little toy my darling knew,
   A little sock of faded hue,
A little lock of golden hair.

Long years ago this holy time,
   My little one — my all to me —
   Sat robed in white upon my knee
And heard the merry Christmas chime.

"Tell me, my little golden-head,
   If Santa Claus should come to-night,
   What shall he bring my baby bright,—
What treasures for my boy?" I said.

And then he named this little toy,
   While in his round and mournful eyes
   There came a look of sweet surprise,
That spake his quiet, trustful joy.

And as he lisped his evening prayer
   He asked the boon with childish grace,
   Then, toddling to the chimney-place,
He hung this little stocking there.

That night, while lengthening shadows crept,
   I saw the white-winged angels come
   With singing to our lowly home
And kiss my darling as he slept.

They must have heard his little prayer,
   For in the morn, with rapturous face,
   He toddled to the chimney-place,
And found this little treasure there.

They came again one Christmas-tide,—
   That angel host, so fair and white!
   And singing all that glorious night,
They lured my darling from my side.

A little sock, a little toy,
   A little lock of golden hair,
   The Christmas music on the air,
A-watching for my baby boy!

But if again that angel train
   And golden-head come back to me,
   To bear me to Eternity,
My watching will not be in vain!

"Great deeds cannot die"

From: *THE PRINCESS:* A Medley *by* ALFRED, LORD TENNYSON

'Alas your Highness breathes full East,' I said,
"On that which leans to you. I know the Prince,
I prize his truth: and then how vast a work
To assail this gray preeminence of man!
You grant me license; might I use it? think;
Ere half be done perchance your life may fail;
Then comes the feebler heiress of your plan,
And takes and ruins all; and thus your pains
May only make that footprint upon sand
Which old-recurring waves of prejudice
Resmooth to nothing: might I dread that you,
With only Fame for spouse and your great deeds
For issue, yet may live in vain, and miss,
Meanwhile, what every woman counts her due,
Love, children, happiness?'

                    And she exclaim'd,
'Peace, you young savage of the Northern wild!
What! tho' your Prince's love were like a God's,
Have we not made ourself the sacrifice?
You are bold indeed: we are not talk'd to thus:
Yet will we say for children, would they grew
Like field-flowers everywhere! we like them well:
But children die; and let me tell you, girl,
Howe'er you babble, *great deeds cannot die;*
They with the sun and moon renew their light
For ever, blessing those that look on them.
Children—that men may pluck them from our hearts,
Kill us with pity, break us with ourselves—
O—children—there is nothing upon earth
More miserable than she that has a son
And sees him err: nor would we work for fame;
Tho' she perhaps might reap the applause of Great,
Who learns the one POU STO whence after-hands
May move the world, tho' she herself effect
But little: wherefore up and act, nor shrink
For fear our solid aim be dissipated
By frail successors. Would, indeed, we had been,
In lieu of many mortal flies, a race
Of giants living, each, a thousand years,
That we might see our own work out, and watch
The sandy footprint harden into stone.'

ADVICE CONCERNING LOW SPIRITS

February 16th, 1820

Dear Lady Georgiana:

Nobody has suffered more from low spirits than I have—so I feel for you and make these suggestions.

1st   Live as well as you dare.

2nd   Go into the shower-bath with a small quantity of water at a temperature low enough to give you a slight sensation of cold—75° or 80°.

3rd   Read amusing books.

4th   Shorten your views of life—not further than dinner to dinner or dinner to tea.

5th   Be as busy as you can.

6th   See as much as you can of those friends who respect and like you.

7th   And of those acquaintances who amuse you.

8th   Make no secret of low spirits to your friends, but talk of them freely — they are always worse for dignified concealment.

9th   Attend to the effects tea and coffee produce upon you.

10th   Compare your lot with that of other people.

11th   Don't expect too much from human life—a sorry business at best.

12th   Avoid poetry, dramatic representations (except comedy), music, serious novels, melancholy sentimental people and everything likely to excite feeling or emotion not ending in active benevolence.

13th   Do good and endeavor to please everybody of every degree.

14th   Be as much as you can in the open air without fatigue.

15th   Make the room where you commonly sit gay and pleasant.

16th Struggle little by little against idleness.

17th Don't be too severe upon yourself, or underrate yourself, but do yourself justice.

18th Keep good blazing fires.

19th Be firm and constant in the exercise of rational religion.

20th Believe me, dear Lady Georgiana,

Very truly yours,
SYDNEY SMITH

* * *

Sixteen Characteristics of Love

1. It is long-suffering.
2.   is kind.
3.   envieth not.
4.   vaunteth not itself.
5.   is not puffed up.
6.   doth not behave itself unseemly.
7.   seeketh not its own.
8.   is not easily provoked.
9.   thinketh no evil.
10.   rejoiceth not in iniquity.
11.   rejoiceth in the truth.
12.   beareth all things.
13.   believeth all things.
14.   hopeth all things.
15.   endureth all things.
16.   never faileth.

St. Paul—I Cor. XIII

Friendship Is a Continuing Certainty

From an essay *by* RALPH WALDO EMERSON

I do then with my friends as I do with my books. I would have them where I can find them, but I seldom use them. We must have society on our own terms, and admit or exclude it on the slightest cause. I can not afford to speak much with my friend. If he is great, he makes me so great that I cannot descend to converse. In the great days, presentiments hover before me, far before me in the firmament. I ought then to dedicate myself to them. I go in that I may seize them. I go out that I may seize them. I fear only that I may lose them receding into the sky, in which now they are only a patch of brighter light. Then, though I prize my friends, I cannot afford to talk with them and study their visions, lest I lose my own. It would indeed give me a certain household joy to quit this lofty seeking, this spiritual astronomy, or search of stars, and come down to warm sympathies with you; but then I know well I shall mourn always the vanishing of my mighty gods. It is true, next week I shall have languid times, when I can well afford to occupy myself with foreign objects; then I shall regret the lost literature of your mind, and wish you were by my side again. But if you come, perhaps you will fill my mind only with new visions, not with yourself, but with your lustres, and I shall not be able any more than now to converse with you. So I will owe to my friends this evanescent intercourse. I will receive from them not what they have, but what they are. They shall give me that which properly they cannot give me, but which radiates from them. But they shall not hold me by any relations less subtle and pure. We will meet as though we met not, and part as though we parted not.

Old Monkish Litany

From twice-cooked food,
From an ignorant doctor,
From a reconciled enemy,
From a wicked woman,
    Lord, deliver us.

In a Thousand Years
(How Times Have Changed)

(A woman's prediction of the future written nearly 100 years ago)

'Twill be all the same in a thousand years!
What a terrible line this, to draw out the tears.
Oh, how oft do I weep at the dance, or the play,
O'er the sorrows we women are doomed to convey;
And can it be so, must we stand at the gate,
Denied all the honors of the country or state?
Our part but to please and obey lordly man;
Be kind when he's surly, and be sweet as we can;
As students to shiver, like leaves in the breeze,
If we chance to infringe on his rules or decrees?
Then have pity, ye gods, who look down on our case,
Shut from Bar, Bench and School Board, and every fat place,
To pick up the pennies that oppressors fling down,
For cutting and stitching, and clothing the town.
Oh, the tyrant's sharp lash, his "pooh poohs" and his sneers,
Will be all the same in a thousand years.

Ah! 'tis not the same in a thousand years;
How sweet and how pleasant our life now appears,
For women no longer bow down to the nod
Of creatures who ruled with a chain and a rod;
But as lawyers they plead, and as doctors dissect,
And in temples of learning control and direct.
The weak footed student at mile-posts may rest
Without springing as mine in the President's breast.
There's no splitting of hairs to deny her the prize,
She receives her diploma and a blessing likewise;
Now women no more stitch and stew for their lives,
Or suffer injustice because daughters or wives;
Lo, they sit down as jurors, they judge and they vote,
And in steering through life ply an oar in the boat.
The mother departed looks down here with pride
On her merciful child dealing charity wide;
While man, that once governed so harsh and severe,
Applies for positions in meekness and fear;
Now the cane of the dude is no more on the street,
The eyeglass is missing, and sharp-pointed feet,
The poor "chappy" himself is beyond the bright spheres,
For 'tis not the same in a thousand years.

The Pattern of Change

by W. E. H. LECKY

Little snatch of ancient song,
What has made thee live so long?
Flying on thy wings of rhyme
Lightly down the depths of time,
Telling nothing strange or rare,
Scarce a thought or image there,
Nothing but the old, old tale
Of a hapless lover's wail;
Off-spring of an idle hour,
Whence has come thy lasting power?
By what term of rhythm or phrase,
By what subtle careless grace,
Can thy music charm our ears
After full three hundred years.

*　*　*

Landmarks of the human mind
One by one are left behind,
And a subtle change is wrought
In the mould and cast of thought;
Modes of reasoning pass away,
Types of beauty lose their sway;
Creeds and causes that have made
Many noble lives must fade,
And the words that thrilled of old
Now seem hueless, dead, and cold;
Fancy's rainbow tints are flying,
Thoughts, like men, are slowly dying;
All things perish, and the strongest
Often do not last the longest;
The stately ship is seen no more,
The fragile skiff attains the shore;
And while the great and wise decay,
And all their trophies pass away,
Some sudden thought, some careless rhyme,
Still floats above the wrecks of Time.

Let This Be a Happy Day

Let this be a day of kind words and helpful deeds. Resolve that this last day of September shall live on through years to come, and that its fragrance shall be like the lingering sweetness of the last rose of summer, perfuming all the air around it.

> If you have a kind word—say it,
>   Throbbing hearts soon sink to rest;
> If you owe a kindness—pay it,
>   Life's sun hurries to the west.
>
> Can you do a kind deed—do it,
>   From despair some soul to save;
> Bless each day as you pass through it,
>   Marching onward to the grave.
>
> Days for deeds are few, my brother,
>   Then to-day fulfil your vow;
> If you mean to help another,
>   Do not dream it—do it now.

ANONYMOUS

> O spirit, be no more content
>   To dream, aspire, and long!
> Grasp thou the grand, the beautiful,
>   The proud, the free, the strong!
> I rouse! no more for far-off good,
>   With folded hands, I pine;
> I seek, I yet *will find,* the springs
>   To quench this thirst divine!
> And these, all these I covet now,
>   God helping, *shall* be mine!

GRACE GREENWOOD

A Ballad of Santa Claus

by HENRY VAN DYKE From *The Grand Canyon*
For the St. Nicholas Society of New York

Among the earliest saints of old, before the
    first Hegira,
I find the one whose name we hold, St. Nicholas
    of Myra:
The best-loved name, I guess, in sacred
    nomenclature,—
The patron-saint of helpfulness, and friendship,
    and good-nature.

A bishop and a preacher too, a famous
    theologian,
He stood against the Arian crew and fought them
    like a Trojan:
But when a poor man told his need and begged
    an alms in trouble,
He never asked about his creed, but quickly gave
    him double.

Three pretty maidens, so they say, were longing
    to be married;
But they were paupers, lack-a-day, and so the
    suitors tarried.
St. Nicholas gave each maid a purse of golden
    ducats chinking,
And then, for better or for worse, they wedded
    quick as winking.

Once, as he sailed, a storm arose; wild waves the
ship surrounded;
The sailors wept and tore their clothes, and
shrieked "We'll all be drownded!"
St. Nicholas never turned a hair; serenely shone
his halo;
He simply said a little prayer, and all the billows
lay low.

The wicked keeper of an inn had three small
urchins taken,
And cut them up in a pickle-bin, and salted them
for bacon.
St. Nicholas came and picked them out, and put
their limbs together,—
They lived, they leaped, they gave a shout, "St.
Nicholas forever!"

And thus it came to pass, you know, that maids
without a nickel,
And sailor-lads when tempest blow, and children
in a pickle,
And every man that's fatherly, and every kindly
matron,
In choosing saints would all agree to call St.
Nicholas patron.

He comes again at Christmas-time and stirs us up
to giving;
He rings the merry bells that chime good-will to
all the living;
He blesses every friendly deed and every free
donation;
He sows the secret, golden seed of love through
all creation.

Our fathers drank to Santa Claus, the sixth of
each December,
And still we keep his feast because his virtues we
remember.
Among the saintly ranks he stood, with smiling
human features,
And said, *"Be good! But not too good to love your
fellow-creatures!"*

December 6, 1907

There Is Nothing Like a Woman

A WOMAN is like to—but stay—
What a woman is like, who can say!
 There's no living with or without one—
 Love bites like a fly,
 Now an ear, now an eye,
 Buz, buz, always buzzing about one.
  When she's tender and kind,
  She is like to my mind,
(And Fanny was so I remember)
  She's like to—Oh dear!
  She's as good very near
As a ripe melting peach in September.
   If she laugh and she chat,
   Play, joke, and all that,
And with smiles and good-humour she met me,
   She's like a rich dish
   Of ven'son or fish,
That cries from the table, come eat me!
But she'll plague you, and vex you,
  Distract and perplex you, and vex you,
  False hearted, and ranging,
  Unsettled and changing,

What then do you think she is like?
          Like a sand? like a rock?
          Like a wheel? like a clock?
      Aye, a clock that is always at strike.
      Her head's like the island folks tell on,
      Which nothing but monkeys can dwell on,
      Her heart's like a lemon—so nice
      She carves for each lover a slice;
          In truth she's to me,
          Like the wind, like the sea,
      Whose raging will hearken to no man;
          Like a mill, like a pill,
          Like a flail, like a whale,
          Like an ass, like a glass,
      Whose image is constant to no man;
          Like a flow'r, like a show'r,
          Like a fly, like a pie,
          Like a pea, like a flea,
          Like a thief, like—in brief,
      She's like nothing on earth—but a woman!

[Note—they did *not* say *Dame*. This dates back to the 18th Century.]

True Love

Love not me for comely grace,
For my pleasing eye or face,
Nor for any outward part,
No, nor for a constant heart:
    For these may fail or turn to ill,
        So thou and I shall sever.
Keep, therefore, a true woman's eye,
And love me still but know not why—
    So hast thou the same reason still
        To doat upon me ever!

Anonymous

*   *   *

If you've anything good to say to a man,
    Don't wait till he's laid to rest,
For the eulogy spoken when hearts are broken
    Is an empty thing at best.

MICHAEL JOSEPH DONNELLY

Smile Through Those Tears

Even a May-day has its shadows. Perhaps the early morning gave promise of calm and sunny skies, but clouds arose and hid all the brightness. But can you not look on and see the results? New flowers will blossom, new streams be flowing, fresh grass be springing and twigs sprouting. Will the earth look dark and gloomy always hereafter? Ah, no! she will be the better for it. And are there clouds in your sky too? Do you feel as if it were December instead of May? It is only a passing storm; don't go about carrying gloom on your face and despair in your heart. Doubtless you feel as if your world were all wrong and your whole life a mistake—not a bit of it! It will all come right, by and by.

If we never saw the contrast that there is 'tween sun
    and rain;
If we never knew the difference that there is 'tween joy
    and pain;
How could we prize the beauty of a sunlit summer day,
Or know half the glowing pleasure of an hour that's
    free and gay?

MABEL PERCY

*   *   *

It is easy enough to be pleasant
    When life flows by like a song,
But the man worth while is the one who will smile
    When everything goes dead wrong;
For the test of the heart is trouble,
    And it always comes with the years,
And the smile that is worth the praises of earth
    Is the smile that shines through tears.

ELLA WHEELER WILCOX

BUSINESS BREVITIES

The Yankee Peddler—
The First American Huckster

by Richardson Wright, from *Hawkers and Walkers in Early America*

In its beginning his life story differed little from that of hundreds of youths and men who found adventure in peddling and who, as forerunners of our domestic commerce, helped to colour and make amusing and mildly picaresque the itinerant life of early America.

Each generation of young Americans has discovered its own vivid, distinctive, and picturesque varations of adventure. Trading with the savage Indian in the depths of the wilderness furnished enough excitement to satisfy the most lusty of youths. Indian wars and wars with other nations gave abundant outlets for the excess energy of young men who dreamed fierce dreams. Between these military forays, many youths found excitement and, incidentally, their business education, along the easier-going—but none the less adventuresome—paths of peaceful commerce that threaded their way from settlement to settlement and penetrated the awesome, virgin stretches of the frontiers.

For a long time in this country an active form of selling goods was peddling. Most of the peddlers, or chapmen, as they were often called, hailed from New England, Connecticut especially.

Their trade fell into various branches. There were the general peddlers, who hawked an assortment of useful "Yankee notions"—pins, needles, hooks and eyes, scissors, razors, combs, coat and vest buttons, spoons, small hardware, children's books, cotton goods, lace and perfume. Besides there were the specialized itinerant dealers – tin-peddlers, clock-peddlers, chair-peddlers, peddlers of spices, essences, dyes, woodenware, pottery, brooms, books, and a host of other items; and even these specialists, as we shall see, often carried several side lines of goods and did many other things beside selling their wares. Sometimes they vended very cumbersome articles – washing machines, spinning wheels, cabinet organs, and winnowing machines and corn shellers. Even wagon-makers hawked their product and they could be met driving through the country with a train of light carts or carriages; and in winter they had a string of sleighs lashed together. There were, in addition, the peddlers on the canals and rivers, and

the wholesale itinerant merchants. A still further distinction can be made between local peddlers with a relatively small route and those who travelled great distances.

The dealer in small wares, essences and such, was called a "trunk-peddler," because he carried his goods in one or two small, oblong, tin trunks slung on his back by a webbing harness or a leather strap.

Although in Colonial times the peddler's stock was limited to a few items, by 1830 it had extended to all sorts of merchandise. Large wagons loaded with drygoods, hats, boots, shoes, clocks, firearms, hardware, and even furniture became a common sight on our country roads.

From house to house the peddler went, from town to town. And quite a flutter he caused when he appeared on the village green and opened his pack. Women dropped their chores and men their work, and gathered about to hear gossip of the neighbourhoods the peddler had recently left, and to see his wares.

A peripatetic merchant, he showed up wherever there was a chance for a sale. Not only did he visit the isolated country homes with his stock of goods, but he managed to be present on market days in town, at vendues or auction sales, on military training days, and at the spring and autumn country fairs.

May and November were the usual months for these fairs, and sometimes they lasted three days. To them farmers brought their horses and cattle for sale and sundry goods of household manufacture. There were sports and bouts of all kinds, accompanied by a noise of blaring trumpets and scratchy fiddles and screeching whistles and of people having a good time.

In the colonial days the Buckthorn Inn, in New York City, displayed, with amazing commercial candor, a sign that read:

> *Four pence a night for a bed*
> *Six pence with supper*
> *No more than five to sleep in one bed*
> *No boots to be worn in bed*
> *Organ grinders to sleep in the wash house*
> *No dogs allowed upstairs.*
> *No beer allowed in the kitchen*
> *No Razor grinders or Tinkers taken in.*

Both young and old, these peddlers played an unforgettable role in the romance of our early widening frontiers. The first commercial move westward was made by Indian traders—the Dutch of New York and the Pennsylvania, who carried goods into the territory lying beyond the fringe of the settlements. The Dutch were trading regularly with the Iroquois at Albany by 1700. But these New Yorkers were not very intrepid merchants. When they reached an advantageous point, they built a fort and a trading post, and the Indians were induced to bring in their pelts for exchange. The Pennsylvanians, on the other hand, were a more adventurous, crafty and chivalrous crowd. Their pack trains crossed the Alleghanies and penetrated to the Ohio and the Wabash in the early years of the eighteenth century. They carried a variety of goods which were bartered for pelts. Now and then, when they could escape the eye of the authorities, they sold arms and ammunition to the Indians. The Pennsylvanian traders also had a line of trading cloth called "duffels" and "strouds." As early as 1727 these hardy Pennsylvanian traders with their pack horses were developing commerce along the Ohio with the Mingoes, Delawares and Shawnees.

When emigrants began to filter into these regions, the old Indian traders—usually Irish and Scotch-Irish—often took to peddling and to pack-training.

While this fur trader was the first commercial agent to make a peaceable penetration of the opening western lands, the Yankee notions-peddler from New England followed on the heels of migration. Whether it was the California Trail or the Oregon, we find him quick to take advantage of these new markets. And he had not only the settlers to sell to, but the Indians as well. One expedition to Oregon in 1832 encountered three vehicles containing a gross of axes for the Indian market, vermilion and other paints, glass beads, small looking-glasses, tawdry trinkets, cheap knives, buttons, nails, hammers, and other articles on which young Indians of both sexes set a high value and white men little or none.

Again and again in the early tales of the expansion of the nation westward and southward, we find travellers making note of these itinerant merchants. They would pop up in the most unexpected places. Even Horn's *Overland Guide to California*—the Baedeker of the forty-niners—contains the advertisement of a Mr. Sypher in Fort Des Moines, who is willing to supply peddlers with drygoods, groceries, hardware, cutlery, caps, boots and shoes, books and stationery, drugs, medicines, paints, oils and dye-stuffs at the lowest possible rates.

In many instances peddling was the means of support by virtue of which migrating settlers made their way to their new homes. An Ephraim Davis (to note one instance out of many) when he reached the age of 21 and was seized with a lust for frontier life, invested his adolescent savings in Yankee notions and, filling two tin trunks, slung them over his shoulder and peddled his way westward across the New England states and up through the Mohawk Valley until, in the autumn of 1791, he reached the spot he planned to settle in. There he made his home, founded the first iron forge and cotton mill in the locality, and served a useful purpose in his chosen spot. His simple annals were brought to a close in 1854.

But there was more to the Yankee peddler's role in the widening of the frontier than the mere selling of goods. These young men with packs on their backs were the forerunners of whole groups that left their New England farms to settle in the new West. They surveyed the possibilities of various regions and, on returning home, reported their findings. They were the scouts for that great migration westward and southward of the hardy New England stock which first peopled the frontiers — part of that half million souls who between the Revolution and 1800 moved into western New York, Virginia, Tennessee, and Kentucky.

Scarcely a town in New England but was represented on the road by one or more itinerants. Meriden, Connecticut, sent thirty to forty of its young men constantly on the roads of the South and the West. From Wolcott, Connecticut, ten youths fared forth every year. Weare, New Hampshire, was represented by fifteen peddlers at one time. Such were the young men who brought back to their New England homes news of the land Manasseh Cutler led his people to in the Marietta region of the Northwest Territory, news of the rich Mississippi Valley, of the wide prairies of Illinois, of the vastness of Texas, and of the possibilities that lay at the ends of the Oregon and California Trails.

The Root of Evil

How blest is he above the many
Who turns today a handsome penny,
By stating to the drowsy throng
The line dividing right and wrong!
For richer pickings he commands
Than ears of corn rubbed in the hands.
How different now from days of yore,
When sandal-shod and spirit sore,
With stiffened joints and limber thews
And garments damp with midnight dews,
The poor Apostles, staff in hand,
Went limping through a stranger's land.
Now charge they up and down the way,
Like jockeys on the Derby Day;
And we poor wights must waltz aside,
And let the pulpit princess glide;
Or have a phaeton o'er us wheeled,
Or have our heels adroitly peeled.

Oh money! money! root and start
Of every sin, 'tis claimed thou art;
But let them doubt the fact who will,
'Tis money spreads the gospel still.

The Story of Building
and Financing
the Cross-Continental Railroads

In July, 1862, Congress, though burdened with the terrific war problem, passed the Pacific Railway Bill authorising the construction of a continuous line from the Missouri River to the Pacific Ocean. Two private companies were then formed to build this line—the Union Pacific for the eastern part and the Central Pacific for the western. These companies were to receive Government aid as follows: 1. A free right of way 400 feet wide. 2. An issue of Government bonds amounting to one half the cost of the road. 3. An absolute gift of ten alternate sections of land per mile (12,800 acres) on each side of the line. 4. Privilege of using coal, iron, etc., from the region through which building operations extended. 5. To receive on completion of continuous sections of 20 miles the bonds of the United States as follows: A. Between the Missouri River and eastern base of mountains, about 650 miles, $16,000 a mile. B. Across the Rocky Mountains, 150 miles, $48,000 a mile. C. Across the Great Basin, $32,000 a mile. D. Across the Sierra Nevada, 150 miles, $48,000 a mile. E. To San Francisco, about 120 miles, $16,000 a mile.

The Government also obliged itself to extinguish the title of Amerinds to all lands donated. The State of California assumed the interest for twenty years on $1,500,000 of the Central Pacific bonds, assistance estimated as the equivalent of $3,000,000 in gold. San Francisco gave $400,000 and Sacramento donated 30 acres of land. The aggregate of land given to the two companies was ten million acres. Thus it seems that the Government practically paid for the whole line. It would have been better if it had built the road without the intervention of the companies. About two miles a day was made in track building, then considered rapid work. The chief contractor was J. S. Casement, and William Dodge was chief engineer. The workmen lived in trains which were pushed ahead as fast as the road advanced and were supplied with plenty of rifles and ammunition for protection against the Sioux and other roaming tribes. These hovered about like vultures, choosing opportune moments for attack. The assistant engineer, P. T. Browne, with his party, was fired on sixty

miles west of North Platte. They fought for about two hours against seventy-five natives. Browne was killed.

Sometimes the American Indians destroyed the track, captured trains, killed engineers, firemen, brakemen, and telegraph linemen. They also would destroy the telegraph line and carry off the wire. In fact, they were a constant terror and menace. But when denouncing them nobody remembers the swindles perpetrated on them in former years, nor the bad whiskey which impoverished them and brutalised them and won their furs for a bagatelle. Their attitude was largely the result of the earlier treatment they had received from the whites, as well as of all the bad white blood which had been infused into the tribes. One of the worst affairs was the Plum Creek massacre. William Thompson, an Englishman, a telegraph man, was sent out with a party of five to hunt up a break. They started about nine o'clock one evening and when they reached the place a pile of ties was discovered on the track for the purpose of wrecking a supply train nearly due. Barely had this discovery been made when Thompson and his men were attacked by the enemy. They fired back and then ran. One of the natives on a horse pursued Thompson, shot him through the arm, and then knocked him down with a clubbed rifle. Next he stabbed him in the neck to finish him, and immediately began the operation of removing Thompson's scalp. As Thompson was far from dead the prospect was not agreeable, but a movement would have brought death. His only chance was to keep quiet and let the work go on, and he was able to do this notwithstanding the pain. But when the scalp was jerked loose he thought his whole head was off, and then felt as if a red-hot iron had been passed over his crown.

The native tucked the scalp in his belt and mounting rode hastily away, but in doing so dropped the scalp and its owner picked it up. Thompson was obliged to remain quiet while the band piled more ties on the track. Presently he heard the distant rumble of the train. It was impossible to do anything to prevent the wreck. In a few moments the cars were piled in a heap. The engineer and fireman were shot and scalped; the train was ransacked by the light of a huge fire. A barrel of whiskey was opened and all got drunk. When daybreak came they set the whole wreck on fire and gleefully danced around it. When they were finally gone from the scene Thompson crawled away and at length reached Willow Island station, where a rescuing party found him. People came from all around to see his ghastly baldness. He was taken to a hotel where a doctor dressed his wound. "In a pail of water was his scalp, about nine inches in length and four in width, somewhat resembling a drowned rat as it floated curled up on the water." Such were the incidents due to the wild tribes which constantly harassed the builders of this iron trail.

But these Indians were little worse than those who composed a large part of the population of each terminus. They had different methods, that was all. Whiskey flowed free and drunkenness was, as usual with our European race, the great recreation. Gambling dives and grog shops made up a large part of the mushroom town that grew up at each official end of the track. All manner of people, like birds of prey, flocked to these places to secure a share of the money paid to the workers, who were numbered by thousands. Some buildings were fairly substantial, but there were many that were merely board sides with a canvas roof. Others were "dugouts," that is, holes in the ground roofed over with sticks and earth; in a side hill if possible. There were large numbers of tents. Where there were vertical clay banks along a dry water course, or a stream, these were burrowed into near the top, a square chamber being made seven or eight feet long, five or six high, and four or five deep, the outer side being closed by a blanket or canvas hung from the upper edge. Rents were high and any shelter at all was valuable.

From time to time, as progress of the line demanded, the official terminus was moved on. From Grand Island it jumped to North Platte, then to Julesburg, then to Cheyenne, and so on, in some cases leaving a permanent town of considerable proportions behind. In the case of Cheyenne a city of five thousand sprang out of nothing, and there were three newspapers; but in some instances the advance left behind only a wreck looking as if a tornado had swept that way. Remnants of old clothes, boards, straw, broken furniture, thousands of tin cans, empty bottles, etc., strewed the ground in all directions. At Green River a number of adobe houses were built, the ruins of which were still standing at the time of my first visit to that locality in 1871. Even two or three miles up the track I found dugouts and a large amount of wreckage to remind one of the late "prosperity." The life at these places had all the most vicious qualities of our civilisation, and few of its good ones. There were no policemen, and the state of disorder may be imagined. It was a feverish nightmare of horrors, in striking contrast to the sobriety of the life the Mormons brought to the Wilderness.

Three years after the beginning of the great work, which it was thought would require ten, the day came when the ceremony was to be performed that should complete the engineering triumph. On May 10, 1869, two engines at Promotory Point, Utah, were brought head to head, a half-world at each

back, as Bret Harte said, only a small space intervening, where the crowd gathered to witness the driving of the last spike which should bring far seas together and mark an end and a beginning. There was a prayer by the Reverend Doctor Todd. The last tie, of California laurel, beautifully polished and bearing on one side a silver plate with names of officers engraved upon it, was then laid. Two rails were next placed opposite each other, one for the Union, the other for the Central Pacific. Following this was a presentation of spikes on the part of California, Nevada, and Arizona. Governor Stanford responded for the Central Pacific, and General Dodge for the Union Pacific. With a silver hammer for driving the last spike, presented by the Union Express Company, Governor Stanford stood on the south rail, while Dr. Durant, to drive another, stood on the north one. At a signal that the telegraph was ready these spikes were driven, the last one, the golden spike of the Central Pacific, being connected with the telegraph so that the strokes of Stanford's hammer were repeated all over the country, and at the final blow "done" was sent to the waiting world. The crowd cheered; Dr. Durant and Governor Stanford shook hands. Telegrams of congratulation were received. General Dodge, the engineer in chief, and Jack and Dan Casement, the chief contractors, were the heroes of the hour. The work was finished.

The operation of building this line partly belongs to the romantic period of Breaking the Wilderness, but when the last spike of gold was sent home and the engines met upon the rails a new and different epoch began. Scarcely less fascinating, up to this moment, have been its events, but this volume is not for them. The trail of the iron horse, which would annihilate the vast distances of the Wilderness, where the life blood of so many had softened the way, was an accomplished fact. The new era was at hand. Europe and Cathay stood at the last face to face, in the midst of that once "northern mystery" which was the dream of the gold-hunting conquistadore. The Seven Cities of Cibola had long ago vanished, but the rich cities of the Republic were building in their place, and wealth beyond the wildest imagination of the early adventures was now to flow from every corner of the broken Wilderness.

Profit Without Risk

In the times of 1836, there dwelt in the pleasant town of T. a smooth oily-mannered gentleman, who diversified a commonplace pursuit by some exciting episodes of finance—dealing occasionally in exchange, buying and selling uncurrent money, &c. We will suppose this gentleman's name to be Thompson. It happened that a Mr. Ripley of North Carolina, was in T., having some $1200, in North Carolina money, and desiring to return to the old North State with his funds, not wishing to encounter the risk of robbery through the Creek country, in which there were rumors of hostilities between the whites and the Indians, he bethought him of buying exchange on Raleigh, as the safest mode of transmitting his money. On inquiry he was referred to Mr. Thompson, as the only person dealing in exchange in that place. He called on Mr. T. and made known his wishes. With his characteristic politeness, Mr. Thompson agreed to accommodate him with a sight bill on his correspondent in Raleigh, charging him the moderate premium of five per cent for it. Mr. Thompson retired into his counting-room, and in a few minutes returned with the bill and a letter, which he delivered to Mr. Ripley, at the same time receiving money from that gentleman plus the exchange. As the interlocutors were exchanging valedictory compliments, it occurred to Mr. Thompson that it would be a favor to him if Mr. Ripley would be so kind as to convey to Mr. T.'s correspondent a package he was desirous of sending, which request Mr. Ripley assured Mr. T. it would afford him great pleasure to comply with. Mr. Thompson then handed Mr. Ripley a package, strongly enveloped and sealed, addressed to the Raleigh Banker, after which the gentlemen parted with many polite expressions of regard and civility.

Arriving without any accident or hindrance at Raleigh, Mr. Ripley's first care was to call on the Banker and present his documents. He found him at his office, presented the bill and letter to him, and requested payment of the former. That, said the Banker, will depend a good deal upon the contents of the package. Opening which, Mr. Ripley found the identical bills, minus the premium, he had paid Mr. T. for his bill: and which the Banker paid over to that gentleman, who was not a little surprised to find that the expert Mr. Thompson had charged him five per cent. for carrying his own money to Raleigh, to avoid the risk and trouble of which he had bought the exchange.

T. used to remark that that was the safest operation, all around, he ever knew. He had got his exchange—the buyer had got his bill and the money, too,—and the drawee was fully protected! There was profit without outlay or risk.

ADVICE TO A SON

by FRANCIS OSBORNE

A few books well studied, and thoroughly digested, nourish the understanding more than hundreds but gargled in the mouth. . . .

Follow not the tedious practice of such as seek Wisdom only in Learning. . . .

The way to elegancy of style is to employ your pen upon every errand; and the more trivial and dry it is, the more brains must be allowed for sauce. . . .

Wear your clothes neat, exceeding rather than coming short of others of like fortune. . . .

Never buy but with ready money; and be drawn rather to fix where you find things cheap and good, than for friendship or acquaintance. . . . If you get nothing else by going from one shop to another, you shall gain experience. . . .

Such as are betrayed by their easy nature, to be ordinary security for their friends, leave so little to themselves, as their liberty remains ever after arbitrary at the will of others. . . .

Honesty treats with the world upon such vast disadvantage, that a pen is often as useful to defend you as a sword, by making writing the witness of your contracts. . . .

Beware . . . of thinking yourself wiser or greater than you are. Pride brake the angels in Heaven, and spoils all heads we find cracked here. . . .

Shun pride and baseness, as tutors to contempt, the first of others, the latter of yourself. . . .

To whisper with another, in company of your betters, is uncivil, and the more eminent the person is, the greater suspicion is raiseth. . . .

When you speak to any (especially of quality) look them full in the face; other gestures bewraying want of breeding, confidence, or honesty. . . .

Impudence is no virtue, yet able to beggar them all; being for the most part in good plight when the rest starve. . . .

Beware what company you keep, since example prevails more than precept. . . .

Let your wit rather serve you for a buckler to defend yourself, by a handsome reply, than the sword to wound others. . . .

Be not the trumpet of your own charity, or vices; for by the one you disoblige the receiver as well as lose your reward; and by the other you alarm the censures of men.

At the age of thirty, sitting in his vessel's cabin, while the wind was still, Emerson wrote these firm sentences without altering a word:

" A man contains all that is needful to his government within himself. He is made a law unto himself."

" All real good and evil that can befall him must be from himself. He only can do himself any good or any harm."

" Nothing can be given to him or taken from him but always there is a compensation."

" There is a correspondence between the human soul and everything that exists in the world; more properly, everything that is known to man."

" Instead of studying things without the principles of them, all may be penetrated unto within him."

" Every act puts the agent in a new condition."

" The purpose of life seems to be to acquaint a man with himself."

" He is not to live to the future as described to him, but to live to the real future by living to the real present."

" Perhaps thy lot in life is higher
Than the Fates assign to me,
While they fulfil thy large desire,
And bid my hopes as visions flee.
But grant me still in joy or sorrow,
In grief or hope, to claim thy heart,
And I will then defy the morrow
Whilst I fulfil a loyal part."

Checkpoints for the Busy Executive

From a speech entitled *The New Type of Executive*
given by J. George Frederick at the Executives' Club of Chicago
April 13, 1928

I have worked out a series of points which I consider the new type of executive must use in his job and thereby do justice to himself and his company. They are:

1. Choose his job, quite as carefully as he becomes chosen.

2. Insist on clearly defining the authority and responsibility before he begins work.

3. That he has professional standards, for his profession, as an executive.

4. That he goes ahead when he knows he is right, but first he makes sure that he knows. This is the thing which is vital to the objective approach.

5. That he discounts experience.

6. That he classifies himself functionally, and not by industry.

7. That he develops complete humility and open-mindedness of judgment. That he specializes as an executive on these things first of all: On picking men, on getting pertinent facts, study them, and translating the facts into operating policies.

8. That he understands the great difference between policy and principle, between fact and opinion, between judgment and counter-checked decision.

I want to stop right here to say that one of the gravest mistakes made in business today, is the confusion between fact and opinion. I find that many men have a vast deal of difficulty in realizing that very vital distinction. They will insist on considering an opinion a fact, or, conversely, considering a fact as an opinion, and they cannot seem to get the more scientific objective point of view, and grasp that great difference between what is a fact and what is an opinion. Kettering of General Motors has a sign in his office: "Opinions will not be tolerated here except when there are no facts available."

9. That he discounts all vanity of power and eliminates hunch judgment and merely judgment decision.

10. That he grasps the vast significance of the law of averages and of statistics. Now, although I am a research man, I am not a statistician. I hate figures, and I think every normal man does. But, as a great publisher, who does business in

many millions, said to me not long ago, "I hate statistics, but I can't do without them." And that is precisely what should be the attitude of every man with regard to statistics. There are some people so statistically minded that they can eat them for breakfast, lunch and supper; they cannot seem to get away from them, they cannot seem to understand that they are a means to an end, not an end in themselves.

There are today, with regard to figures and statistics, two seriously mistaken attitudes. One is an under-valuation of statistics. And the other is an over-valuation of statistics. It seems to be difficult for many men to strike that normal, sane balance in statistics which gives them the proper point of view as to the use of statistics, without either over-valuing or under-valuing them.

11. That he leaves to others the matters of today, and concentrates on the issues of tomorrow. That is another very vital factor in the new type of executive. An executive has absolutely no business having on his desk one single thing that has to do with today. A good executive will mark as a demerit upon himself every time that he finds himself working on things that have to do with today.

12. That he understands the vital nature of strategy and time annihilation in business. Now, what I mean by strategy and time annihilation is this: As in military affairs, strategy in business is the primary consideration always. In other words, there is a strategy of time, place, and circumstance, which can only be synthesized in the brain of a high type of executive. A sound policy may be unsound from a strategic point of view, when all the facts are focused into a strategic judgment.

A WESTERN BOY'S LAMENT
by Eugene Field

I wish't I lived away down East, where codfish salt the sea,
And where the folks have pumpkin pie and apple-sass for tea.
Us boys who's livin' here out West don't get more'n half a show;
We don't have nothin' else to do but jest to sort of grow.

Oh, if I was a bird I'd fly a million miles away
To where they feed their boys on pork and beans three times a day;
To where the place they call the Hub gives out its shiny spokes,
And where the folks—so father says—is mostly women-folks.

ENIGMA

That elusive thing called "Time"

The lightest and the softest thing
That floats upon the zephyr's wing,
I move with unresisting ease,
Before the breath of every breeze.

With power resistless and sublime,
I sweep along from clime to clime,
And I defy all earthly force
To intercept me in my course.

A favorite guest with all the fair,
I play with Beauty's twisted hair;
And harmless as the gentlest dove,
I share the couch of happy love.

'Tis mine to hurl the bolts of fate,
That overwhelm the guilty great;
I wield the giant arm that brings
Dismay and death on tyrant kings.

No throb of passion ever pressed
The vacant chambers of my breast;
And no desire nor dream of care
Could ever gain admittance there.

With passion's various fires I burn;
And all, as each prevails in turn,
With equal rage incessant roll
Their boiling currents through my soul.

In Folly's lap I had my birth,
The simplest creature on the earth;
At Folly's bosom I was nursed,
And am as simple as at first.

The wisest own that I am wiser,
And sages make me their adviser;
The great demand my prudent cares,
To aid them in their state affairs.

I boast but little outward grace,
For frequent stains deform my face;
And when I bathe, though strange it seems,
I seek from choice the foulest streams.

I soar to fields of liquid light,
Where rainbows glow and stars are bright;
I sun me at their spotless fires,
And sport amid the heavenly choirs.

The nameless being of a day,
I barely am, and pass away;
Nor leave a trace behind, to be
The record of my history.

No chance or change has power enough
To harm my life's perennial stuff;
For I have built my throne sublime
Upon the wreck of conquered Time.

Is This the American Image Today?

by E. W. HOWE From *Ventures in Common Sense*
written in 1919

Our Puritan culture, as every one knows, makes for many laudable virtues: enterprise, industry, philoprogenitiveness, patriotism, the fear of God, a great appetite for brummagem ideals, a high desire to be righteous, a noble gratitude for the fact that we are not as other men are. But one of the things it does *not* make for is that austere intellectual passion which exalts a bald fact above comfort, security and the revelation of God — one of the things it does *not* promote is common truthfulness.

The American, indeed, always views the truth a bit suspiciously, particularly if it be the truth about himself and his; he seems convinced that it is dangerous, and perhaps downright indecent. There is in him none of the Slav's habit of merciless introspection, none of the Frenchman's penetrating realism, none of the German's appetite for putting the bitter facts of life into hair-raising axioms. In his philosophizing he roams the superficial, leaping back almost blushingly every time his foot upturns the fundamental. It is words that always fetch him, not realities; he is the most abject slave of mellifluous and meaningless phrases ever on view in the world. And, since words and phrases, however lovely, have a way of failing when they are put to the test, he forces himself inevitably into a sort of preposterous dualism. On the one side is the moony philosophy he serves with the lip; on the other side is the harsh, realistic, Philistine philosophy he actually practices. On the one side is the ethic that meets the national notion of propriety; on the other side is the ethic that practically works. This disparity between what is publicly approved and what is privately done is at the heart of theAnglo-Saxon, and especially of the American character; it sets our people off from nearly all other peoples. It is the cause of the astounding hypocrisy that foreigners always see in us, both when we denounce them and when we seek to court them, and it is the cause, too, of our national inability to understand those foreigners and their habits of mind.

That hypocrisy, to the foreign eye, bathes the American scene; even the more civilized varieties of Englishmen are acutely conscious of it. We posture as apostles of fair play, as good sportsmen, as professional knights errant—and throw beer-bottles at the umpire when he refuses to cheat for our side. We bawl about malefactions of Big Business—and every man in Little Business is trying to gouge and rob his way into Big Business as fast as he can. We save the black-and-tan republics from their native Bryans, Roosevelts and Burlesons—and flood them with "deserving Democrats" of our own. We deafen the world with our whoops for liberty—and submit to laws that invade and destroy our most sacred rights.

No wonder foreigners stand amazed before the incredible contrast between our pretention and our practice—men jailed for republishing parts of the Bible and the Declaration of Independence, notorious drunkards advocating prohibition on the floor of Congress, bawdy judges sentencing men under the Mann Act, shyster lawyers lifted into office as reformers, trust-busting politicians borrowing money from trust magnates, tax-dodgers exposing and denouncing tax-dodgers, uplifters picking the public pocket, *pleureurs* for democracy abolishing democracy, men imprisoned, knocked about, tortured in the land of liberty for daring to speak out for liberty.

What lies under all this, of course, is easy enough to see. The primary difficulty is that the American people, despite a century and a half of struggles for freedom, are still burdened by a crushing heritage of Puritanical pishposh, and that it forces them into efforts to obey rules of conduct which no healthy race could actually observe and survive. The secondary difficulty is to be found in the extraordinary timorousness, the pervasive intellectual cowardice, which Puritanism carries with it. The thing needed is obviously a thorough overhauling of the outworn national code—perhaps its forthright abandonment and the formulation of an entirely new one, closer to the unescapable facts. But that is precisely what Americans seem least fitted for. The impulse that revealed itself in a Machiavelli, in a Montaigne and in a Nietzsche, and that shows itself even to-day, on a lower scale, in a Wells and a Shaw, is apparently not in them. Such a man, rising among them, would be smothered in distrust, and perhaps swiftly conducted to the calaboose; there is no country in the world in which iconoclasm is more perilous. Rather than grapple with the fundamental problem, the American prefers to confine himself to superficialities, and what he accomplishes on that plane is usually no more than a clumsy rearrangement of the old platitudes. A glance at even the most serious American newspaper is sufficient to show how shallow American thinking is—how much a matter of mere formulae, most of them palpably unworkable and idiotic. And if that glance were not enough, a study of the gigantic literature of "inspiration," so peculiar to the country, would furnish proof enough. That literature is devoted ardently and fatuously to reconciling the dualism I have mentioned; it seeks to perfume the practical philosophy of the land by finding justification for it in the theoretical philosophy; it is a huge effort to reconcile the "good" man and the man who, Yankee fashion, gets on in the world. In politics and government the clash is particularly visible. There is no country in which legislation directs itself toward loftier goals and is more sharply flavored with pious purpose, and there is no country in which the manner of its enactment is more corrupt and dishonest, or in which there is a larger body of unenforced and unenforceable laws.

Ten Short Hints for Men of Business
1830

1. Pursue the business you are engaged in with zeal and avidity. Without much industry and energy, your time will melt away with little or no profit. It follows from this obvious rule that you ought to concentrate your attention upon one particular line of business, rather than distract it among several. If you have many different irons in the fire, some of them will most probably burn.

2. Mind your own concerns; do not trust implicitly to agents or clerks. If you wish anything well done, you must either do it yourself, or *see* it done by others. Even your agent will soon learn to despise you, as well as neglect your concerns, unless you show an interest in them yourself. Attend to your business, and he will attend to it. Neglect it yourself, your agent will neglect it. If he does not, take that man to your heart; he is one man out of ten thousand.

3. It naturally flows from the last rule, that you must rise early to see the course of your business The man who wastes the first moments of the day in bed is sure to produce the same habit among all those who live within the range of his influence.

4. In all cases prefer your business to your pleasures. The former not only suffers from your neglect, but your reputation as a man of punctuality and industry suffers with it.

5. Let your credit always keep pace with your capital. Never stretch it, but on some great emergency, lest you snap it. Let the world see that you would rather make slow and sure gains than venture some risks—that you labor rather than gamble in your vocations. Besides, in these dashing enterprises, a man not only risks his own credit, but taxes the good humor of his friends.

6. When you are under the necessity of appealing to your friends, you ought never to ask it, unless you in your turn incur an equal responsibility for them, or make them secure by a pledge of property.

7. Make no important agreement, unless you reduce it to writing. Men may prove scoundrels; or their memories, at least, may prove treacherous. The ink will remain as it is; but words, volatile words will fly away and be forgotten. Nearly a fourth of the causes that lumber our dockets proceed from neglect of this obvious rule. Besides, death may sweep off one of the parties, and the other may be at the utmost loss to prove the existence or terms of the bargain.

8. Observe the utmost order in the prosecution of your business. Enter every debt or credit as it occurs. Beware of the foul fiend Ennui, and mind the good maxim, to do everything while you think of it. Have a place for everything, and let everything be in its place—more especially your papers, for more is lost, and vexation incurred by a hunt after some straggling document, than is generally conceived. Have a place for all papers to be attended to; and particularly for all letters to be answered—for your correspondents will think themselves affronted by a want of punctuality.

9. Take a receipt for all monies you pay, or any debts, in whatever way you discharge them. These receipts must not be taken on loose bits of paper which may be mislaid from their place, or lost from their file. For what injury may not arise from their loss? To remedy this inconvenience I earnestly advise you to have a large blank-book set apart for the purpose of registering your receipts.

10. As nearly as possible, settle your accounts at least once a year.

A Business Man's Thoughts
Two Generations Ago

BY E. W. HOWE

1. The only real human motive is intelligent self-interest; altruism is not only bogus, but impossible.

2. The first object of self-interest is to survive. The possession of money makes it easier to survive. *Ergo*, it is virtuous to get money.

3. A man who gets it is a better citizen than one who doesn't; what he does for himself also benefits the community in general.

4. The aim of all reformers is to get something for themselves. They pretend that it isn't; hence, even when they chance to serve good causes, they are liars.

5. Any American of average talents and decent industry can get enough money, barring acts of God, to make himself comfortable.

6. Any man who fails to do so shows an unfitness to survive, and deserves to be exploited by his betters.

7. The people have a remedy for all public abuses in their hands. If they fail to get relief, then the blame lies wholly upon their own credulity, emotionalism and imbecility.

8. One secret has been kept many centuries: the terrible worthlessness of the people collectively. Bad government is like a worthless young man whose folks are rich, and who put up money to hide his mistakes.

9. One of the dangerous men in public life is the orator and writer who is sent on a mission at public expense, and who returns with a false report.

10. There is always a type of man who says he loves his fellow men, and expects to make a living at it.

11. All should have ideals they cannot quite reach; all should be a little high-minded, and accomplish some of the greater

good, but it is business men who know these things may be made professional and mischievous. In thousands of years there has been no advance in public morals, in philosophy, religion or in politics, but the advance in business has been the greatest miracle the world has ever known.

12. I can't give the man working for me as much as he thinks he is entitled to: I can only pay him what he earns, and my obligation to him is no greater than his obligation to me. I am entitled to as much credit for giving him work as he is entitled to credit for working; I am as much a working man as he is, as honest, and equally entitled to protection and respect.

13. There may have been a time when employers were overbearing, but they are not now; they have been punished so much that in nine cases out of ten they are willing to make every possible concession.

14. Any one who bets on his judgment against the judgment of the world, will be punished for folly. In everything in which man is interested, the world knows what is best for him. It has learned from experience, best of all teachers. Millions of men have lived millions of years, and tried everything. The results of these experiments have passed down from the first to the last generation. Everywhere there is an undercurrent of truth that any one may take advantage of; whatever hypocrites may say, there are enough burned children to warn you to keep your hand out of the fire. One trouble with every one is conceit; we all have a natural disposition to know it all, and to trust our judgment against experience. Look over the next fool you meet; even you can tell him how to avoid most of his troubles. Those persons who teach sentiment —who make hope better than it is—are doing harm; and there are millions of them. Good judgment and good taste are big chiefs which will never fail to help you.

Fences Are Only for Those Who Cannot Jump

by Eugene Whitmore

In every walk of life, in every job, in every organization there are "fences." Sometimes these fences are very real—again, only imaginary.

These fences are useful in defining limits, in dividing and assigning work, and in setting policies. The trouble is, in many cases the person, the company or the organization outgrows the fence.

When this happens, great rewards come to the man or woman who has the nerve to "jump the fence." An excellent illustration of what happens when someone jumps the fence is in the variety store field. For half a century Woolworth, Kresge, Kress and other variety store organizations were members of an association of limited-price variety stores. They first sold only items which cost five and ten cents. Then someone jumped the fence and they began selling items up to one dollar.

For many years no one tried to sell these variety stores anything to retail at more than a dollar. Then one jumped the fence, kicked off the restraints and started running. Today the variety stores sell items priced at $100 and up. They are bigger, more prosperous than ever before.

Somewhat the same thing happened in the soft-drink field. For three quarters of a century all soft drinks came in six-ounce bottles, mainly because the most popular drink was sold in such bottles. The fences—in this case, wholly imaginary—held back an entire industry. Once again the lid blew off when someone began selling soft drinks in larger bottles, and a whole new sales area was opened. New companies entered the field when the oldest and largest company adopted larger bottles.

There was another fence around the soft-drink business. Everyone was convinced that to be popular a soft drink had to be sweet—oh, so sweet. A daring person decided that some people would prefer a soft drink with less sugar content. Along came Seven-Up, Sprite and perhaps two dozen other drinks which were not quite so sweet, had fewer calories, and were more palatable to millions of people. Another fence was ground into the earth. The sweet soft drinks still sell in multi-million bottle quantities every year, but the man who jumped the fence and brought out soft drinks which are slightly, ever so slightly, tart opened a whole new field for sales.

One of the world's greatest "fence busters" is Sears Roebuck and Company, the world's greatest retail merchandising organization. Someone recently said, "We have millions of retailers in this country and only one Sears Roebuck." This great company might be accused of—credited with, would be a better term—continuous experimentation.

As the mail-order business grew up, there came to be all sorts of "fences" in, through and around it. One fence was "cash with order." Sears Roebuck smashed that fence and quickly proved that something like ninety-nine per cent of all Americans will pay their bills and meet installment payments promptly.

There were other fences in the mail-order business—one was that only farmers and other rural people would buy from a mail-order house. But that was wrong. Years ago an analysis of mail-order sales showed that Pennsylvania, an important industrial as well as agricultural state, led all others in the number of mail-order customers per thousand population.

Sears Roebuck developed methods by which customers could be insured of a reasonably satisfactory fit when buying items like coats, suits, trousers, hats, shoes and shirts. The same company prepared instructions to help people put up their own wallpaper and then sold not only more wallpaper but the tools to go with it.

There was a time when Sears Roebuck refused to sell seeds or plants or shrubs because they could not guarantee that they would grow. Once more, someone jumped the fence and put Sears into the seed, plant and shrub business in a big way. One of the earliest Sears Roebuck stores was on Lawrence Avenue in Chicago, some ten miles from the parent plant on the West side. Experimentally, the store manager rented a vacant lot near the store and stocked it with a small assortment of rose bushes, seeds, flowering plants, shrubs and trees. Before anyone realized what had happened, the lot was crowded with eager buyers and the store manager was howling for more merchandise. Down went another fence.

When Sears began opening retail stores, people said, "Town and city people don't know Sears Roebuck, and their retail stores will fail." Ever since that date in the mid-twenties when Sears experimentally opened its retail stores, fences have been crashing down all over the world. Doubting Thomases said Sears could never operate successfully in Mexico and other Latin American countries where age-old custom decrees that buyer and seller haggle over prices. But in one area after another, when Sears opened big stores in Mexico, people came in droves to buy everything in sight without once attempting to beat down the marked prices.

I have tried for years to find an example of leadership which was not built and did not grow without crashing through some kind of fence. So far I have been unsuccessful. Every business with which I am familiar had to knock down fences before it could make a place for itself.

Until a few years ago every shoe manufacturer in this country was content to make footwear, period. Then along came Maxie Jarman, a Tennessee genius whose father had started a small shoe factory in Nashville and prospered modestly. At that time, traditional shoe stores did a huge business fall and winter, spring and summer, leaving big gaps in sales between seasons. Like other shoe manufacturers, Mr. Jarman started a chain of retail shoe stores because of the need to level out production. While he did not originate the idea of a manufacturer owning retail outlets, he did develop it on a large scale. Then he decided it was possible for a shoe manufacturer to produce apparel which would clothe men, women and children from head to foot, and from the skin out.

Here was another bold exercise in fence jumping. Hundreds of other manufacturers asserted "the shoe business is different," declaring it impossible for a shoe manufacturer to make underwear, coats, suits, foundation garments and also to operate department stores.

Well, Mr. Jarman's several companies, all part of Genesco (derived from the company's earlier corporate name of General Shoe Company) now operate clothing, underwear, foundation garment factories, operate department stores, and are doing right well, thank you.

As usually happens, other shoe companies are now getting into the act with the purchase of department store chains, work clothing and other factories. But it was, so far as we are able to determine, Maxie Jarman who took the first jump over the old fence that had kept shoe manufacturers in a tight, little corral.

How does the "jump the fence" principle apply to individuals employed in large companies? We often hear people complain that today business is so big and so tightly organized that earning promotion to executive jobs is increasingly difficult. Not so.

Business is compartmented, make no mistake about that. There is the story about two men discussing National Biscuit Company and one said that NBC was so big it had a vice-president in charge of Fig Newtons. The other man did not believe it and telephoned National Biscuit Company. When he asked for the vice-president in charge of Fig Newtons, so the story goes, back came the query from the telephone operator, "Packaged or bulk?"

How do you jump fences, win promotion to executive jobs in business today? Well, here's one way. Conrad Ohlendorf, a teller in a small bank, had a smile for every depositor. When small depositors brought in an unusually large deposit, he complimented them. Each person who walked up to his window he made feel that his business was appreciated. Officers noted that more people went to his station than to others. Then one day the board of directors called in Mr. Ohlendorf and said, "Conrad, we have appointed you vice-president and loan officer."

Often it is just as simple as that. Do your job just a mite better than average and first thing you know someone will help you jump a fence.

More than six hundred different makes of automobiles have been manufactured in the United States since the turn of the century. Why, out of all this great assortment of cars, is there only one Cadillac?

How many companies in America manufacture hats? And why is there only one Stetson? Why has no one been able to duplicate the success of Hershey bars, Wrigley's chewing gum, Ivory soap, Corona typewriters, National Cash Registers, Sara Lee bakery products, IBM accounting machines and computers?

In each of these—and other cases—where one product or one company's product undeniably dominates the field, there were high fences which, at times, seemed to bar the company's or the product's progress.

When salesmen first went out to sell cash registers, merchants and businessmen and especially employees considered it an insult to suggest a machine which recorded sales. Of course, the machine was fought vigorously by dishonest employees but also by honest ones who thought the machine was a reflection on their integrity.

Cash register salesmen were thrown bodily out of stores, insulted, asked to leave, told to get out and stay out. All sorts of fences were erected against the sale of cash registers. But every fence was jumped. And today a merchant is considered a bad credit risk if he doesn't have cash registers to protect his business, each individual sales person, and the customer against mistakes or occasional dishonesty.

Neither the telephone nor the air brake met with quick success. Railroad men said that George Westinghouse was insane to think that air could stop a moving freight train with many tons of cars and freight and the vast momentum it generated under speed. But air did stop trains and eventually no train was allowed to move without air brakes.

A British writer said that a factory had no more need for a telephone than for a balloon. More than one hundred manufacturers of buggies refused to believe that a gasoline engine would ever replace the horse. They went to the wall, still believing that automobiles were a rich man's toy.

When we investigate why no other washing machine manufacturer has been able to match the performance of Maytag, we find a story about founder F. L. Maytag. He had started in business in a tiny factory in Newton, Iowa, where he made an attachment for harvesting machines. When a farmer reported something wrong with one of these attachments, Mr. Maytag hurried to the first train bound for the farmer's town, hired a horse and buggy, drove to the farm and personally repaired the broken part of his attachment.

Superior service to customers has persisted down through the years and become a part of Maytag policy and tradition. No "fence" was high enough to prevent F. L. Maytag from rushing to a customer in trouble. It would have been easy to tell the farmer-customer to get his machine repaired at the local blacksmith shop, or that the guarantee had expired, or to have hidden behind any one of a dozen "fences" some manufacturers erect between their guarantee and actual performance. But not Mr. Maytag. When he heard of one of his products not working, all he could think of was getting that item back in working order.

One night last winter we were having late dinner in a midwestern restaurant. Outside a blizzard raged and only a few customers were in the dining room. Suddenly, something went wrong with the cash register and in a short time, probably fifteen minutes, a man came in, wearing heavy boots and a huge coat still covered with snow, and carrying the little tool kit that identified him as the National Cash Register service man.

In a few minutes he had that register back in working order and was on his way through the blinding blizzard, possibly to another call. This is but one of the reasons why there is only one company which has been consistently successful in the cash-register business.

Other makers of cash registers have spent millions in an attempt to cut into this lucrative field. They could not because the founder and his successors at Dayton, where the chief cash-register factory is situated, have never let a fence—real or imaginary—stop them from serving customers better than any competitor dared to attempt.

A few years ago a Chicagoan started baking a coffee cake which he called Sara Lee. Said to be the most expensive commercially-made coffee cake on the market, it was priced as much as twice that of other coffee cakes sold in stores and bakeries.

"He'll lose his shirt," said a dozen or more big-scale bakers whose coffee cakes sold for much less. "People will never pay his prices."

First thing anyone knew Sara Lee coffee cakes were selling out almost as soon as a shipment was delivered to a store. Demand soared skyward. And before long it was necessary to build the largest, most modern, most highly automated coffee cake bakery in the world.

The Sara Lee coffee cake baker had jumped all sorts of fences—some of them labeled "price"— in his march to leadership. If he had faltered at any one "fence", there would be no Sara Lee brand today. Instead, he jumped every fence that confronted him.

Early in his career, William Wrigley had an offer from what was then called the "chewing gum trust." The top management of this outfit told Mr. Wrigley that they would pay him a good price for his business and when he refused to sell, they intimated they had plenty of money, some well-known brands and would soon put him out of business if he did not sell. What did Wrigley answer?

"I am going to take your business away from you!"

The chewing gum moguls in astonishment assured Mr. Wrigley that with all their power, he could not possibly take their business. But William Wrigley Jr. just laughed and said,

"Yes, I am going to take your business away from you—one stick at a time." And he did just that.

How did he do it? With a superior product, superior service to every customer, and a firm policy of improvement and innovation at every step of his career. His son and now his grandson have meticulously followed the broad, constructive outlines of William Wrigley's earliest policies. And though many changes have occurred since the business' early days, the basic policies of top quality and strict attention to customer needs have never been altered.

When Milton Snavely Hershey, founder of the Hershey Chocolate Company, began marketing his Hershey bars, it was customary in the candy business to sell every merchant—no matter how small—as much candy as possible. Candy, especially chocolate candy, is perishable. In warm weather it may turn gray, which, though it in no way lessens the quality of the candy, is unappealing to the consumer. Candy makers of those days did not bother about candy which deteriorated in dealer stocks, saying that since the dealer bought it, it was his problem.

Hershey jumped that "fence" by instructing his salesmen not to sell a customer more candy than he could move before it deteriorated, if only in appearance. Many were the times an early Hershey salesman cut down an order offered by a customer.

Did this policy pay Mr. Hershey? Well, ask yourself. Do you know any other candy bar similar to Hershey's that has reached first base in the national market? Many have tried manfully to imitate and sell a Hershey bar. None has succeeded. Why? Because they let a lot of "fences" stand in their way while Mr. Hershey jumped every fence he encountered.

Years ago, the president of a small Ohio food company drove into a service station for gasoline. He noticed that the young station man was reading a book on salesmanship.

"Where did you get that book?" asked the manufacturer.

"At a second-hand book store."

"Are you finding it interesting?"

"Yes, sir. I'm going to be a salesman someday."

"How would you like to come work for me?"

That brief conversation led to the young man's employment as a salesman with the food company. He made a splendid record, rose to be sales manager and when the company merged with a much larger competitor, the erstwhile service station attendant became vice-president in charge of sales for the combined company.

To thousands of young men who work in service stations there are all varieties of "fences" to keep them from winning advancement. But this young man jumped all the fences, using a second-hand book as a springboard.

Two young men were employed in the sales department of a well-known company. One resigned his job because he said that since it was a family-owned company there was no chance for advancement for those outside the clan which owned the majority of the company's stock.

The other young man stayed on and made such a record that he became the first non-member of the family to become president. It turned out that the family "fence" could easily be jumped after one son became a medical man, another a lawyer, and neither of the grandsons wanted to be actively associated with the family company.

In every position you may hold there will seem to be tall "fences" hemming you into a static job with little future. At times it will seem that the only thing to do is to go with another company. But wherever you go you will find fences, real or imaginary. So it may be, and often is, better to stay where you are and jump the fences instead of running away from them.

Many years ago a man named Thomas D. Murphy owned a small newspaper in Red Oak, Iowa. When Montgomery County, Iowa, built a new courthouse in the then-current style with gables, steeples, domes and a high-pitched roof, he obtained a woodcut of the new structure. Printing it on a large sheet, he attached to the bottom a calendar pad for the year—1890— then sold local ads to circle the picture.

While hundreds of county courthouses were a-building over the country at the time, only Mr. Murphy thought of using a picture of one with an attached calendar pad. And only Mr. Murphy thought of selling advertisements on the calendar.

Soon he had salesmen visiting every town in the country where citizens were proud of a new courthouse. Eventually, when they ran out of courthouses, Murphy substituted pictures of pretty girls, sea and moutain scenes. And this was how the calendar business was born.

One of Mr. Murphy's salesmen was Herbert H. Bigelow who founded the famed Brown & Bigelow Company, St. Paul. Bigelow was a man who never stopped at high fences. He simply jumped them. Every year he put out a new line of calendars and every year he had something different and better. To do this, he paid famous artists well for pictures; he imported presses to obtain special printing results.

Although Mr. Bigelow died many years ago, no other calendar company has approached Brown & Bigelow in size.

Probably the best comment on "fences" ever uttered was the remark made by the late E. C. Simmons, a pioneer in selling and marketing and founder of the great Simmons Hardware wholesale empire.

A company man came to Mr. Simmons one day, complaining that other people in the organization were interfering—"buttin' in," as he put it—in his department. And would Mr. Simmons define his authority and tell other people to respect it?

"All right," said Mr. Simmons, "I will build a fence around your department to keep other people out of it. But that same fence will keep you inside it—and away from all chance of promotion."

Have respect for fences. Use them when they are needed. But remember that every successful person, every successful company, had at one time or another—to jump the fence.

*   *   *

It is time to be old,
To take in sail: —
The god of bounds,
Who sets to seas a shore,
Came to me in his fatal rounds,
And said: no more!
As the bird trims her to the gale,
I trim myself to the storm of time,
I man the rudder, reef the sail,
Obey the voice at eve obeyed at prime. . . .

from " Terminus " by Emerson

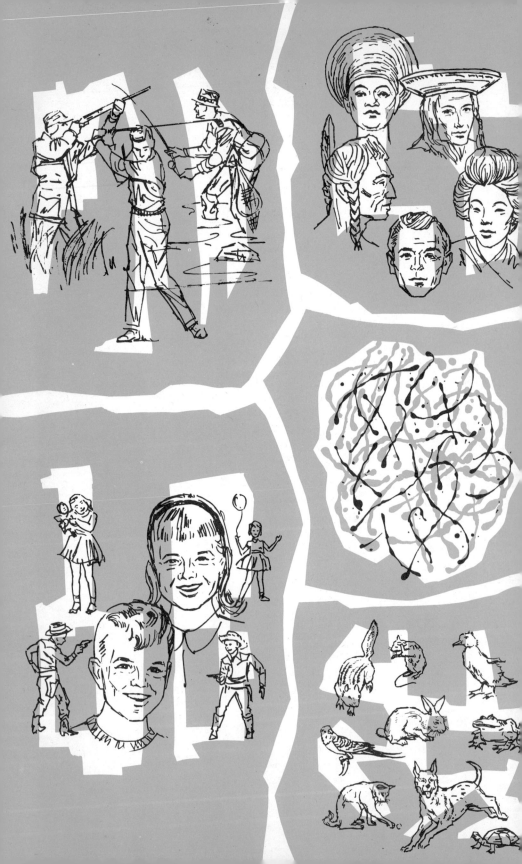